LANGUAGE ARTS
INSTANT ASSESSMENTS
for Data Tracking

Grade 3

Credits
Author: Amy Payne

Visit *carsondellosa.com* for correlations to Common Core, state, national, and Canadian provincial standards.

Carson-Dellosa Publishing, LLC
PO Box 35665
Greensboro, NC 27425 USA
carsondellosa.com

978-1-4838-3618-8
01-339161151

Table of Contents

✦ Assessment and Data Tracking ✦

Data tracking is an essential element in modern classrooms. Teachers are often required to capture student learning through both formative and summative assessments. They then must use the results to guide teaching, remediation, and lesson planning and provide feedback to students, parents, and administrators. Because time is always at a premium in the classroom, it is vital that teachers have the assessments they need at their fingertips. The assessments need to be suited to the skill being assessed as well as adapted to the stage in the learning process. This is true for an informal checkup at the end of a lesson or a formal assessment at the end of a unit.

This book will provide the tools and assessments needed to determine your students' level of mastery throughout the school year. The assessments are both formal and informal and include a variety of formats—pretests and posttests, flash cards, prompt cards, traditional tests, and exit tickets. Often, there are several assessment options for a single skill or concept to allow you the greatest flexibility when assessing understanding. Simply select the assessment that best fits your needs, or use them all to create a comprehensive set of assessments for before, during, and after learning.

Incorporate Instant Assessments into your daily plans to streamline the data-tracking process and keep the focus on student mastery and growth.

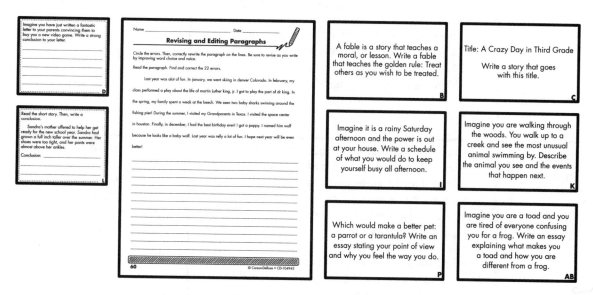

A variety of instant assessments for writing

Types of Assessment

Assessment usually has a negative association because it brings to mind tedious pencil-and-paper tests and grading. However, it can take on many different forms and be a positive, integral part of the year. Not all assessments need to be formal, nor do they all need to be graded. Choose the type of assessment to use based on the information you need to gather. Then, you can decide if or how it should be graded.

	What Does It Look Like?	**Examples**
Formative Assessment	• occurs during learning • is administered frequently • is usually informal and not graded • identifies areas of improvement • provides immediate feedback so a student can make adjustments promptly, if needed • allows teachers to rethink strategies, lesson content, etc., based on current student performance • is process-focused • has the most impact on a student's performance	• in-class observations • exit tickets • reflections and journaling • homework • student-teacher conferences • student self-evaluations
Interim Assessment	• occurs occasionally • is more formal and usually graded • feedback is not immediate, though still fairly quick • helps teachers identify gaps in teaching and areas for remediation • often includes performance assessments, which are individualized, authentic, and performance-based in order to evaluate higher-level thinking skills	• in-class observations • exit tickets • reflections and journaling • homework • student-teacher conferences • student self-evaluations
Summative Assessment	• occurs once learning is considered complete • the information is used by the teacher and school for broader purposes • takes time to return a grade or score • can be used to compare a student's performance to others • is product-focused • has the least impact on a student's performance since there are few or no opportunities for retesting	• cumulative projects • final portfolios • quarterly testing • end-of-the-year testing • standardized testing

How to Use This Book

The assessments in this book follow a few different formats, depending on the skill or concept being assessed. Use the descriptions below to familiarize yourself with each unique format and get the most out of Instant Assessments all year long.

Show What You Know

Most anchors begin with two *Show What You Know* tests. They follow the same format with the same types of questions, so they can be used as a pretest and posttest that can be directly compared to show growth. Or, use one as a test at the end of a unit and use the second version as a retest for students after remediation.

Exit Tickets

Most anchors end with exit tickets that cover the variety of concepts within the anchor. Exit tickets are very targeted questions designed to assess understanding of specific skills, so they are ideal formative assessments to use at the end of a lesson. Exit tickets do not have space for student names, allowing teachers to gather information on the entire class without placing pressure on individual students. If desired, have students write their names or initials on the back of the tickets. Other uses for exit tickets include the following:

- Use the back of each ticket for longer answers, fuller explanations, or extension questions. If needed, students can staple them to larger sheets of paper.
- They can also be used for warm-ups or to find out what students know before a lesson.
- Use the generic exit tickets on pages 7 and 8 for any concept you want to assess. Be sure to fill in any blanks before copying.
- Laminate them and place them in a language arts center as task cards.
- Use them to play Scoot or a similar review game at the end of a unit.
- Choose several to create a targeted assessment for a skill or set of skills.

Word Lists

Word lists consist of several collections of grade-appropriate words in areas that students need to be assessed in, such as sight words, spelling patterns, and words with affixes. They are not comprehensive but are intended to make creating your own assessments simpler. Use the word lists to create vocabulary tests, word decoding fluency tests, spelling lists, etc., for the year.

Cards

Use the cards as prompts for one-on-one conferencing. Simply copy the cards, cut them apart, and follow the directions preceding each set of cards. Use the lettering to keep track of which cards a student has interacted with.

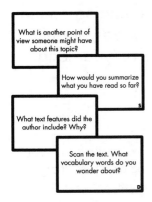

- Copy on card stock and/or laminate for durability.
- Punch holes in the top left corners and place the cards on a book ring to make them easily accessible.
- Copy the sets on different colors of paper to keep them easily separated or to distinguish different sections within a set of cards.
- Easily differentiate by using different amounts or levels of cards to assess a student.
- Write the answers on the backs of cards to create self-checking flash cards.
- Place them in a language arts center as task cards or matching activities.
- Use them to play Scoot or a similar review game at the end of a unit.

Assessment Pages

The reproducible assessment pages are intended for use as a standard test of a skill. Use them in conjunction with other types of assessment to get a full picture of a student's level of understanding. They can also be used for review or homework.

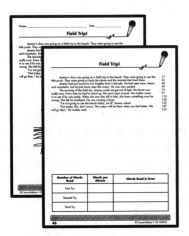

Fluency Pages

Use the paired fluency pages to assess students' oral reading fluency. Provide a copy of the student page to the student, and use the teacher copy to track how far the student read, which words he or she struggled with, and the student's performance on repeated readings. The word count is provided at the end of each line for easy totaling. Then, use the related comprehension questions to assess the student's understanding of what he or she read.

Exit Tickets

Exit tickets are a useful formative assessment tool that you can easily work into your day. You can choose to use a single exit ticket at the end of the day or at the end of each lesson. Simply choose a ticket below and make one copy for each student. Then, have students complete the prompt and present them to you as their ticket out of the door. Use the student responses to gauge overall learning, create small remediation groups, or target areas for reteaching. A blank exit ticket is included on page 8 so you can create your own exit tickets as well.

What stuck with you today?

_____

_____

_____

_____

_____

List three facts you learned today. Put them in order from most important to least important.

1. _____

2. _____

3. _____

The first thing I'll tell my family about today is

_____

_____

_____

_____ .

The most important thing I learned today is

_____

_____

_____

_____

_____ .

Color the face that shows how you feel about understanding today's lesson.

Explain why. _____

_____

Summarize today's lesson in 10 words or less.

_____

_____

_____

_____

One example of _____ is

_____

_____

_____

_____ .

One question I still have is _____

_____

_____

_____

_____ .

How will understanding _____

_____

help you in real life? _____

_____

_____

_____

One new word I learned today is

_____ .

It means _____

_____

_____

_____ .

Draw a picture related to the lesson. Add a caption.

_____

_____

_____

If today's lesson were a song, the title would

be _____

_____

because _____

_____

_____ .

The answer is _____ .

What is the question? _____

_____

_____

_____

_____

Show What You Know
Reading: Literature

Read the story. Then, answer the questions.

Dad's Trumpet

Owen's dad played the trumpet when he was in school. He led the marching band and had a solo in every concert. Owen wanted to play the trumpet too. One day at Grandma's house, he found a dusty case in the closet of his dad's old room. It was Dad's old trumpet! Grandma said that Owen could try it out, so Owen put the instrument to his lips. He blew as hard as he could, but there was no sound. Grandma showed him how to **buzz** his lips on the mouthpiece, and finally the trumpet made a noise. It sounded nothing like the players Owen had heard in the band. Owen felt sad. He guessed he did not have his dad's talent. He was about to put the trumpet away when Grandma stopped him. She smiled and said, "You sound just like your dad did when he first started playing. Don't give up yet!"

1. What character trait does Grandma show? Use text evidence to support your answer.

_____

_____

_____

2. How can you tell that Dad does not play the trumpet anymore?

_____

3. Why does Owen want to learn how to play the trumpet?

_____

4. Buzz is an example of which type of figurative language?
   A. personification
   B. onomatopoeia
   C. hyperbole
   D. simile

5. What is the central message of the story?

_____

_____

Name _____ Date _____

Show What You Know
Reading: Literature

Read the story. Then, answer the questions.

Training Jake

Lucy had a playful dog named Jake. He liked to grab her toys and run away from her. When Jake was a puppy, it was easy to catch him. As Jake grew bigger, Lucy had to shout for him to come back. Neither of them was having much fun. Lucy's mom thought Jake should go to obedience training. A trainer could show Lucy how to teach Jake to obey her. Lucy found a class that met at the park on Saturday mornings. She walked Jake down to the park, but she felt as if Jake was walking her! He was so strong, she could hardly hold him back. At the park, the other dogs were already sitting politely in a circle. The trainer smiled when Jake and Lucy ran up. The trainer said, "Jake is like a brand new battery; he has a lot of energy! I can help both of you learn how to control it."

1. What character trait does Lucy show? Use text evidence to support your answer.

_____

_____

2. How can you tell that training will be good for both Jake and Lucy?

_____

3. Why does Lucy want to train Jake?

_____

4. Read the following sentence from the story:

"Jake is like a brand new battery; he has a lot of energy!"

This is an example of what type of figurative language?

A. hyperbole

B. simile

C. metaphor

D. personification

5. What is the central message of the story?

_____

_____

Before, During, and After Reading Prompts

Use the prompts to assess the class's or an individual student's proficiency with reading comprehension of literature. Choose a card to read aloud. Or, choose several cards to create a whole-class assessment. You can assess a student's pre-reading strategies by using the before reading cards (A–N). During reading, challenge students with the during reading cards (O–AD). When students are finished reading, use the after reading cards (AE–AT) to assess their understanding.

Read the title. What do you think this passage will be about? **A**	Do you think this story will be serious or funny? Why? **B**
What do you think is going to happen in this story? **C**	Do you think you will like this story? Why or why not? **D**
What strategies will you use while reading this story? **E**	What illustrations do you think the author should include? **F**

Based on the title of the story, what character traits would you give the main character?

G

Does the title remind you of any stories you have read before? Which ones?

H

Scan the text and pick out the hardest word to read. How do you say this word? What do you think it means?

I

What are three questions you hope to have answered by reading this text?

J

What strategy can you use if you get stuck on a word while reading this story?

K

What strategy can you use if you have trouble understanding what you are reading?

L

What genre do you think this story is? Why?

M

Why do you think the author wrote this story?

N

What has happened
so far?

O

Who are the main
characters?

P

What is the setting
of the story?

Q

What do you think will
happen next? Why?

R

What is the problem in the
story? How do you think
it will be solved?

S

Do you agree with the
main character's decisions?
Why or why not?

T

How has the main
character affected the
story so far?

U

If the setting were to
change, how would the
story change?

V

What genre is this story? How do you know?

W

What is the author's purpose for writing this story?

X

How do you think this story is going to end?

Y

If you were the main character, what is something you would do differently?

Z

What other story are you reminded of?

AA

Have you ever had something similar happen to you? Explain.

AB

What are two questions you hope to be able to answer by the end of the story?

AC

Why do you think the character is acting the way he or she is?

AD

What lesson does this fable teach?

AE

Explain how the main character feels at the beginning, middle, and end of the story.

AF

Explain why the character did _____.

AG

At first, how does the character feel about _____? How does he or she feel about it later?

AH

What lesson does the main character learn?

AI

Is there something that the main character could have done differently?

AJ

What is the theme or central message of the story? How do you know?

AK

What did you learn by reading this story?

AL

Explain why _____ is important to the characters.

AM

Identify a simile or metaphor used in the story. Explain what it means.

AN

How do _____'s character traits help him or her _____ throughout the story?

AO

Explain what the character does when he or she thinks something is wrong.

AP

Describe how you know _____ and _____ are friends.

AQ

Give a summary of the story.

AR

What is a new word that you learned in the story? What does it mean?

AS

What is the author's point of view about _____?

AT

Name _____ Date _____

Key Details

Read the story. Then, answer the questions.

The Long Hike

Jorge and his friends decided to go on a hike Saturday morning. They wanted to reach the top of a nearby hill so that they could see the whole town. His dad asked if he had remembered to pack water and a snack for the trail. Jorge was in a hurry, but he stopped to pick up a bottle of water and a packet of trail mix for his backpack. He thought they would be back before he got thirsty or hungry, but it took them more time to get to the top of the hill than he had expected. When they stopped to rest, he heard his stomach growl. The view was nice. Jorge and his friends sat down and ate the snack. When they finished, they jogged down the trail. When they got to the bottom of the hill, Jorge saw his mom's car pull up. She rolled down the window and said with a smile, "Are you ready for lunch?" Jorge and his friends all yelled at the same time, "You bet!" Then, Jorge's mom took them out to eat.

1. Which of the following character traits would you use to describe Jorge?

responsible   thoughtful   lazy   unfriendly

2. What effect did the unexpected length of the hike have on the friends?

_____

_____

3. How would the story have changed if Jorge's mom had not pulled up in her car?

_____

_____

4. Complete the flow chart.

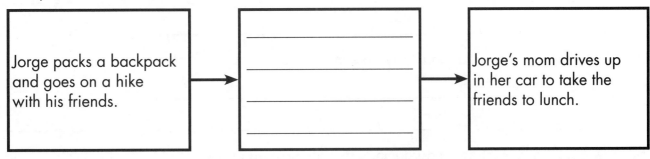

| Jorge packs a backpack and goes on a hike with his friends. | → | _____ _____ _____ _____ | → | Jorge's mom drives up in her car to take the friends to lunch. |

5. What is another good title for this story? Use details from the text to support your answer.

_____

_____

Name _____ Date _____

Making Inferences

Read the story. Then, answer the questions.

Lamar's Tomato Garden

One day, Lamar's class took a field trip to a greenhouse. The students were amazed at how many different plants were growing in the building. They saw plump tomatoes and lovely pink orchids. The gardener explained that she kept the greenhouse warm and misty so that the plants could grow better. She said that it was easier to grow plants inside the greenhouse, where they were not in danger from bad weather or pests. When Lamar got home from school, he told his mother all about the greenhouse. He asked if they could build one in their backyard. Wouldn't it be great to have fresh tomatoes year-round? Mom said, "A greenhouse sounds like fun, but it can be a lot of work. Why don't you grow some tomatoes in a pot first to see if you have a **green thumb**?" Lamar decided to try. He would grow so many tomatoes that they would need a greenhouse to hold them all!

1. What is easier about growing plants in a greenhouse?

_____

_____

2. "Why don't you grow some tomatoes in a pot first to see if you have a **green thumb**?" What does it mean to have a **green thumb**?

   A. Your thumb turns green.

   B. You like to eat tomatoes.

   C. You are good at growing things.

   D. Your parents will build a greenhouse.

3. Explain how a greenhouse would allow you to have fresh tomatoes year-round.

_____

_____

4. What effect does a warm and misty greenhouse have on plants?

_____

_____

5. How does Lamar feel about gardening? Explain how you know.

_____

_____

Character Traits

Read the story. Then, answer the questions.

Dad's Day

Dad's birthday was in June, near Father's Day. Sometimes, they were even on the same day. Isabelle and Hector thought it was unfair when their dad only had one special day in June. Their friends' dads had Father's Day parties in June and birthday parties in different months. Isabelle thought of a way to fix this problem. They would surprise Dad in autumn with Dad's Day. Hector talked to their mom about cooking a special breakfast. She showed him how to cook eggs and bacon. Isabelle made a special card for Dad. They were careful to keep their plans secret. One day in October, Isabelle and Hector woke up early and crept downstairs. They cooked Dad's breakfast and took it upstairs with their card. Dad loved his surprise. He said that he hoped they could have Dad's Day every weekend!

1. What problem do the characters have?

_____

2. What character traits do Isabelle and Hector show in the story?

_____

3. Which of the following is a logical conclusion to the story?

    A. Isabelle and Hector have a Dad's Day every weekend.

    B. Mom teaches Isabelle and Hector how to make bacon and eggs.

    C. Isabelle and Hector oversleep in the morning.

    D. Dad has his birthday party in the autumn too.

4. "Isabelle and Hector woke up early and crept downstairs." Why did they creep downstairs?

_____

_____

5. Based on Isabelle and Hector's character traits, what do you think the special card said?

_____

Story Events

Read the story. Then, answer the questions.

Alicia's Song

Alicia had been practicing for weeks. She sang in the shower, in her bedroom, and on the way to school. Her teacher said that she was ready to sing in a concert, but Alicia was not sure. Mom had taken her to buy a new dress. She helped Alicia curl her hair. Alicia thought she would feel calm when she walked out onstage, but her palms were sweaty, and her shoes felt too tight. She hoped she would not forget the words. Alicia heard the applause for the performer before her. Her friend Chelsea walked off the stage and whispered, "You're on!" Chelsea patted Alicia's shoulder and said, "Good luck!" Alicia took a deep breath and walked into the spotlight. Finally, it was time for her solo. She saw Mom and her teacher smiling at her from the front row and knew she would do well.

1. What is Alicia doing?

    A. dancing

    B. singing

    C. studying

    D. writing

2. Which clues tell you how Alicia feels?

_____

_____

3. How did Mom help Alicia prepare?

_____

_____

4. What does Chelsea do to help Alicia?

_____

_____

5. How does Alicia feel at the end of the story? How do you know?

_____

_____

Plot and Organization

Read the story. Then, answer the questions.

Family Photos

Malia's father had accepted a new job across the country. He would be leaving soon. Malia and her mother would stay in their old house until school was out. Malia would miss her friends when they moved, but she would miss her dad more. Her mother pretended to be cheerful, but Malia knew she would be lonely too. Sometimes, she caught her mom looking at old photos with a tear in her eye. Malia decided to make something that would remind both her mom and her dad that they had a strong family.

One afternoon, Malia took the box of family photos up to her room. She cut out two large cardboard hearts. Then, she picked out pictures of herself, her mom, and her dad. She glued the pictures to the hearts. At the top of each heart she wrote "A Family Is Love." Now, Dad would have pictures to remember them by, and Mom would not be so sad when she looked at the photos.

1. What is Malia's problem?

_____

2. How does Malia try to solve her problem?

_____

3. What is the climax or turning point of the story?

_____

4. How is the second paragraph organized?

    A. Cause and Effect

    B. Sequence

    C. Compare and Contrast

    D. Description

5. Why will Mom be less sad when she looks at the photos?

_____

Name _____ Date _____

Understanding Poetry

Read the poem. Then, answer the questions.

Bubble Gum Bubble

Chew, chew, chew
Puff, puff, puff
Pop! Pop! Pop!

First I chew it like a cow,
I chew and chew
I know you know how

Next I flatten it with my tongue
I puff and puff
Make a bubble using my lung

The bubble grows and grows
Until it goes POP!...
The gum splats upon my nose!

I peel it off, and count to ten
Yummy, yum
Here I go again!

1. This poem is organized into five _____ .

    A. paragraphs   B. stanzas

    C. ideas   D. refrains

2. *Chew*, *puff*, and *pop* are all examples of _____ .

    A. personification   B. hyperbole

    C. simile   D. onomatopoeia

3. Which line contains a simile?

_____

4. What is the poem mostly about?

_____

_____

5. What is another good title for this poem?

_____

A

Bored with Bamboo: A Panda's Story

What do you think this book is about?

_____

B

Write one thing you liked about the story.

_____

Write one new thing you learned.

_____

Write one question you have.

_____

C

Main Idea

Supporting Detail	Supporting Detail
_____	_____
_____	_____
_____	_____

D

Fable (title) _____

The moral of the story is_____

_____ .

I know this because _____

_____ .

E

What do you think the main character looked like? Draw a picture.

F

Main character (name) _____

Two traits _____ _____

How would the story change if the main character were different?

_____

_____

G

Read each phrase. Circle either _literal_ or _nonliteral_.

Don't rock the boat!

literal   nonliteral

Has the cat got your tongue?

literal   nonliteral

Where is the cake pan?

literal   nonliteral

H

Date: _____

New Word: _____

Definition: _____

Strategy: _____

How it helped: _____

_____

Match the genres to their parts.

book   act

drama   chapter

poem   stanza

Name a (book, play, poem) you like.

_____

I

Number the chapter titles in the correct order.

_____ Fluffy Is Scared

_____ The Big Ladder

_____ Fluffy Climbs a Tree

_____ Fluffy Is Home Again

J

Janelle is excited about the weekend. Her birthday party is on Saturday at the zoo!

Point of View: (circle one)

1st Person   2nd Person   3rd Person

Rewrite a line from the story in a different POV.

_____

_____

K

Sammy's New Friend

Why did the author include this illustration?

_____

_____

Circle the most likely genre.

poetry   fantasy

nonfiction

L

Describe the setting of this story.

_____

_____

It reminds me of the setting in another story

called _____ because

_____

M

Rate your reading.

1 I couldn't read it.

2 I needed help.

3 I read most of it.

4 I read it by myself.

N

Title _____

Would you recommend this story to a friend?

Yes   **No**

Why or why not?

_____

_____

O

Color the face that shows how you feel about this text.

Explain. _____

P

✦ Show What You Know ✦
Reading: Informational Text

Read the story. Then, answer the questions.

Delightful Dolphins

Dolphins are thought to be among the most intelligent animals. They are friendly and social animals. They travel in groups, or **pods**, of 10 to 15 dolphins. Scientists believe that dolphins have names for themselves and others. They each have their own whistle sounds. Dolphins recognize their own and other dolphins' whistles, or names, when they hear them. Dolphins seem to like people. They often follow fishing and tour boats. Is this because of the treats people throw from the boats? Maybe. But, it is hard to ignore the big smiles on their faces.

Dolphins talk to each other by clicking, whistling, and making other sounds. They have excellent hearing. They use **echolocation** to find food and other things. Dolphins send out sound waves that are like clicks. When the sound waves hit something, the vibrations bounce back.

Dolphins are amazing. These mammals are among the most loved animals in the world.

1. What kind of animals are dolphins?

_____

2. What is a synonym for **pod**, as it is used in this story?

_____

What is a different meaning for the word **pod**?

_____

3. Write six adjectives found in this text.

_____   _____   _____

_____   _____   _____

4. What is **echolocation** and why do dolphins use it?

_____

_____

5. Why does the author think dolphins are amazing?

_____

_____

Name _____ Date _____

Show What You Know
Reading: Informational Text

Read the story. Then, answer the questions.

Silkworms

Silk is a soft, smooth type of cloth that is used for clothing, bedding, and wall hangings. It comes from silkworm cocoons, which are spun into thread that is then made into cloth. It takes about 3,000 cocoons to make one pound (about 0.5 kg) of silk. Silkworms become moths as adults. Like most insects, silkworms go through four phases, or **stages**. The moth lays its eggs on a mulberry leaf. After a silkworm hatches into a caterpillar, it munches on leaves until it grows to about the length of a human finger. After about a month of eating and growing, the worm spins a cocoon of silk around itself. Spinning the cocoon takes about three days. Inside the **cocoon**, the silkworm changes shape and becomes a pupa. After about three weeks, the pupa turns into a moth. The moth comes out of the cocoon and starts the cycle all over again.

1. What kind of animal is a silkworm? _____

2. What is a synonym for **stages** as it is used in this story?

_____

What is a different meaning for the word **stage**?

_____

3. Write six verbs found in this story.

_____   _____   _____

_____   _____   _____

4. What is a **cocoon** and why do silkworms use it?

_____

5. Why did the author write this text?

_____

Before, During, and After Reading Prompts

Use the prompts to assess the class's or an individual student's proficiency with informational reading comprehension. Choose a card to read aloud. Or, choose several cards to create a whole-class assessment. You can assess a student's pre-reading strategies by using the before reading cards (A–N). During reading, challenge students with the during reading cards (O–AD). When students are finished reading, use the after reading cards (AE–AT) to assess their understanding.

What is the topic of this text? **A**	Based on the title, what do you already know? **B**
Do you think this text is informational or a how-to? Why? **C**	Scan the text. What vocabulary words do you wonder about? **D**
What would you like to learn about this topic? **E**	How do you think the text will be organized? **F**

Why do you think _____ is important?

G

Do you think you will enjoy this text? Why or why not?

H

What other texts have you read about this topic?

I

Where might you look to find background information about this topic?

J

Who do you know that might be very interested in _____?

K

How does this topic make you feel?

L

What text features did the author include? Why?

M

What do you already know about the topic?

N

What will you do when you come to an unfamiliar word?

O

What can you do if part of the text is confusing?

P

What text feature has been helpful as you are reading?

Q

How would you describe the topic of this text?

R

How would you summarize what you have read so far?

S

What are two clues from the text that help you know what _____ means?

T

What questions did you have in the beginning that have now been answered?

U

How did the _____ [text feature] help you understand the text so far?

V

What does this text remind you of? Why?

W

What are two facts you have read so far?

X

What is one question you hope is answered before the end of the text?

Y

What is another word for _____?

Z

Based on what you have read so far, how does the author feel about _____?

AA

How does _____ compare to _____?

AB

What text features should the author have included in the text? Why?

AC

What boldfaced word did the author include in the text? Why did he or she include it?

AD

What is another good title for this text?

AE

What is the main idea of this text? What supporting details are given?

AF

How is this text organized? How do you know?

AG

Why did the author write this text? How do you know?

AH

What steps are involved in _____?

AI

How would you summarize the text?

AJ

Why might an author include more facts than opinions in an informational text?

AK

What is another point of view someone might have about this topic?

AL

What is the order of the events that take place in this text?

AM

How is the author's point of view similar or different to your own point of view?

AN

What is one cause and effect from the text?

AO

What are four facts from the text?

AP

What is another topic this author might write about? How do you know?

AQ

What are two questions you still have about this topic?

AR

What text feature was most helpful? Why?

AS

What subheadings could the author have included in the text?

AT

Main Idea and Supporting Details

Read the story. Then, answer the questions.

Saguaro Cactus

In the Arizona desert, a cactus grows that will live 100 years or more. The saguaro cactus grows very slowly in the hot, dry desert, and it becomes home to many animals as it grows.

The cactus starts as a seed dropped from the fruit of a mature saguaro cactus. The seed sprouts after a rare rain gives it moisture. It swells up, splits its shell, and sends a root down into the soil. Then, the seed sends up a stem.

It does not rain often in the desert, so the stem grows slowly. After one year, it will have grown less than half an inch (1 cm). After 10 years, it may be only 6 inches (15 cm) tall. When it is 50 years old, the original stem is about 15 feet (4.5 m) tall. After 50 years, the saguaro cactus finally grows its first branches.

Many animals make their homes in the saguaro cactus. Animals like its moist skin. Animals such as woodpeckers, mice, hawks, and owls can live in the cactus.

Beautiful flowers grow on the mature saguaro cactus. The flowers provide juicy nectar for birds, insects, and bats. After the flowers dry up, green fruits cover the cactus. Many animals come to eat the fruit. They spread the seeds from the fruit onto the ground where the seeds wait for rain. Eventually these seeds will sprout and grow new saguaro cacti. The cycle will continue for hundreds of years.

1. Why do woodpeckers, mice, hawks, and owls make their homes in saguaro cacti?

_____

2. What causes the cactus stem to grow so slowly?

_____

3. What is the main idea of the text? _____

List three supporting details. _____

_____

_____

4. How is the text organized?
- A. sequence
- B. cause and effect
- C. compare and contrast
- D. description

5. How do new saguaro cacti grow? _____

_____

Cause and Effect

Read the story. Then, answer the questions.

Musical Cultures

People from different cultures celebrate different holidays. They eat different kinds of food. They also have different musical cultures.

The United States has many musical traditions. People in New Orleans, Louisiana, in the southern part of the United States, are known for jazz. This music has strong rhythms. Jazz allows people to play freely. People from a region of the eastern United States called Appalachia play folk music with fiddles and banjos. Much of this music is based on the songs and dance tunes of the British Isles.

Countries that border each other have music styles from the people who cross from one country to the other. Some styles from Mexico are *banda* and *cumbia*. Some Canadian styles of music are based on French songs. These styles use accordions and guitars. Because of radio and TV, people all over the world can hear music of other cultures and create new musical traditions of their own.

1. What is the main idea of this story?

   A. Different cultures have different holidays and food.

   B. Some Canadian music is based on French songs.

   C. People have different musical cultures.

2. What effect did the British Isles have on music?

_____

3. What causes music to change near borders?

_____

4. How do radio and TV affect musical cultures?

_____

5. Explain how you know that this text is organized by comparing.

_____

_____

Point of View

Read the story. Then, answer the questions.

The Olympic Games

People from all over the world take part in the Olympic Games. They gather to compete in different sports. The original Olympics were held in Greece around 776 BC. They occurred every four years. Young men ran races of different lengths. Winners were given wreaths of olive branches.

The modern Olympics resumed in 1896. That year, they were held in Greece. In 1996, people decided to split the Olympic Games. Now, the summer and winter Olympics are held separately. The Olympics now occur every two years. People from more than 200 countries compete in either summer or winter sports. Today's winners receive gold, silver, or bronze medals. They compete in hundreds of events.

The Olympics are good for the host countries too. It gives them a chance to show off their **culture**. Both the people who attend and the people who watch on TV learn about the host country. The sports may differ from the original Olympics, but the spirit of goodwill and good sportsmanship is still the same.

1. Compare the original Olympics to the modern Olympics.

_____

_____

_____

2. When and where were the first Olympics held?

_____

3. What does the author say about how the Olympics help people learn about different cultures?

_____

_____

4. How does the author feel about the Olympics?

_____

5. The author uses the word **culture** in this story. Culture can include a lot of things about a group of people. What does it not include?

    A. music   B. language   C. clothing   D. air

Key Details

Read the story. Then, answer the questions.

Magnets

A magnet is any object with a **magnetic** field. This means that it pulls things made of iron, steel, or nickel toward it. If you set a paper clip next to a magnet on a table, the paper clip will move toward the magnet. Every magnet has what is called a north pole and a south pole. The north pole of one magnet will stick to the south pole of another magnet. If you try to push the south poles of two magnets together, they will spring apart. Earth has magnetic poles too. Earth is a big magnet! Earth's magnetic poles are not actual places. They are areas of Earth's magnetic field with a certain property. Although Earth's magnetic poles are different than the poles where polar bears live, its magnetic poles are near these poles. The north pole of a magnet will always try to point toward Earth's north magnetic pole. A compass is a piece of camping equipment that shows direction. It has a magnetized needle. This needle points to Earth's magnetic north pole. So, if you get lost, pull out your compass and set it on a flat surface. Wait for the needle to point north.

1. What does **magnetic** mean?

_____

2. What happens if you push two south poles together?

_____

3. How does a compass work?

_____

_____

4. What did you learn about the Earth and magnetic poles?

_____

_____

5. Which if the following objects will be affected by a magnet?
   A. a key
   B. a rubber ball
   C. a ruler
   D. a marble

Vocabulary

Read the story. Then, answer the questions.

Reptiles and Amphibians

You may think that lizards and frogs are in the same **family**. They are not! They are actually quite different. Lizards, snakes, turtles, and crocodiles are **reptiles**. Frogs, toads, and salamanders are **amphibians**. Both amphibians and reptiles are cold-blooded. Cold-blooded animals depend on their surroundings for their body temperature. Most amphibians and reptiles lay eggs instead of giving birth to their young. Reptiles lay hard-shelled eggs in nests. Amphibians lay soft-shelled eggs underwater. When reptiles hatch, they look like tiny adults. Amphibian babies might not. Baby frogs, called tadpoles, have to live underwater until they are older. Reptiles feel dry and scaly to the touch. Amphibians feel moist and sticky. Adult amphibians spend their time both in water and on land. This makes amphibians more at risk for becoming sick from pollution. It is important to keep ponds and lakes clean so that the animals that live there will be safe.

1. How are amphibians and reptiles similar?

_____

2. Write a definition for the word **amphibian**.

_____

_____

3. Write a definition for the word **reptile**.

_____

_____

4. Reread the first sentence of this story. What is another word or phrase with the same meaning as **family**?

    A. related siblings

    B. geckos and toads

    C. parents or grandparents

    D. related species

5. How did the boldfaced words help with the comprehension of this text?

_____

_____

Citing Text Evidence

Read the story. Then, answer the questions.

Science Experiments

Scientists learn about the world by conducting experiments. They take careful notes on the supplies they use and the results they find. They share their findings with others. This leads to everyone learning a little more. You can do experiments too! The library has many books with safe experiments for students. You might work with balloons, water, or baking soda. You might learn about how light travels. You might find out why marbles roll down a ramp.

Ask an adult to help you set up your experiment. Let him watch to make sure you are being safe. Be sure to wash your hands afterward. And, remember to clean up the area. Take good notes on your work. You may be able to change just one thing the next time. This might give you a completely different result. Do not worry if your results are not what you expected. Some of the greatest scientific discoveries were made by mistake!

1. What does the author think about science experiments? How do you know?

_____

_____

2. Where can you find information about safe experiments?

_____

_____

3. Should you worry if you get different results? Why or why not?

_____

_____

4. Which sentence(s) do you think a good scientist would NOT say?
   A. "I don't have to write that down. I'm sure I will remember it."
   B. "I should double-check my measurements."
   C. "I'm not going to bother to measure this water."
   D. "It worked once, so I don't have to do it again."

5. Describe how the second paragraph is organized.

_____

_____

A

Write a question that you think you would be able to answer after reading this article.

_____

B

Write **MI** by the main idea. Write **SD** by the supporting details.

_____ It is created when warm air meets cold air.

_____ A tornado is a funnel cloud that forms over land.

_____ It can leave a trail of damage one mile long.

_____ A tornado can form quickly.

C

Circle the words that refer to a sequence of events.

because   so   first   finally

next   after   near   as a result

in conclusion   then   once   tomorrow

D

Write the definition of the boldfaced word as it is used in each sentence.

1. We didn't have recess because of the **weather** outside.

_____

2. Whether you can sing or not, karaoke is fun!

_____

E

Explain why an author might include boldfaced words in a nonfiction text.

_____

_____

_____

_____

F

Title: _____

What is the author's point of view about the topic?

_____

What is your point of view about the topic?

_____

G

Explain how a diagram is designed to help you understand a topic.

_____

_____

_____

_____

H

Title _____

| Cause _____ | → | Effect _____ |

I

Title of Text 1 _____

Title of Text 2 _____

Similar: _____

_____

Different: _____

_____

J

Title _____

Who? _____

What? _____

When? _____

Where? _____

Why? _____

K

Detail _____ +

Detail _____ +

Detail _____ =

Main Idea _____

_____

L

Title of Biography: _____
Complete the time line based on the events in the text.

◄━━━━━━━━━┼━━━━━━━━━┼━━━━━━━━━►

M

Choose a boldface word from the text to answer the questions.

1. What does the word _____ mean?

_____

2. What clues helped you find the meaning?

_____

3. Write a sentence using the word.

_____

N

Frog
- Lives near water
- Amphibian
- Smooth skin
- Poison glands

Toad
- Amphibian
- Dry, bumpy skin
- Lives on land
- Poison glands

Use the pictures and captions to compare and contrast frogs and toads on the back of this exit ticket.

O

DAILY NEWS
The Rain forests are in Danger

Why did the author write this article? Explain how you know. _____

_____

P

Write an imaginary title of a book for each genre.

Biography _____

Autobiography _____

Reference _____

Nonfiction Science _____

✦ Show What You Know ✦
Reading: Foundational Skills

1. Complete each word using a blend or digraph from the word bank. You may use each one once.

cl	ft	nt	ou	ow	st	sw	th

Ty _____ood up and pulled on his _____eater. Today, he and his friends are going to

_____imb a m_____ntain. They are looking for a special fl_____er with one

_____orn. Once they find it, they will spend the rest of the weekend camping in te_____s

and ra_____ing down the river. It will be so much fun!

2. Circle each prefix or suffix. Write the meaning of the underlined word.

A. The teacher asked the students to <u>preread</u> the questions before reading the passage.

_____

B. Please make sure you do not <u>misspell</u> the word *neighbor* on the spelling test.

_____

C. I didn't hear the directions, so I asked the teacher to <u>repeat</u> them.

_____

D. Jules was <u>unable</u> to go outside and play until her homework was done.

_____

E. The <u>thoughtful</u> friends helped him with the tough assignment.

_____

3. Read the sentences. Divide the underlined word into syllables.

A. Taylor is <u>actively</u> trying to win the soccer game right now.

B. The plot of the story was a little <u>confusing</u>, so Sam reread it.

C. The <u>obedient</u> dog would sit, stay, and roll over.

D. I had no trouble <u>convincing</u> my parents to let me spend the night.

4. Circle the misspelled words. Write them correctly below.

On wensday, Kyle went to buy new close to where on his vacashun. The whether was going to be warm with lots of son. He new he wanted to by a swimsoot and flip-flops. He wasn't shure what else he shuld get thow.

_____ _____ _____ _____ _____

_____ _____ _____ _____ _____

Name _____   Date _____

✦ Show What You Know ✦
Reading: Foundational Skills

1. Complete each word using a blend or digraph from the word bank. You may use each one once.

bl	ch	cr	dr	dr	fl	sh	sh	st

Brandy and her family _____ove to the bea_____ for the day. When they got there, they spread a _____anket on the ground. Then, they went searching for sea_____ells in the water. Brandy saw a _____ab and a cuddlefi_____ swimming. Then, she watched a _____ick _____ift by on the waves. The waves got bigger and bigger. They began to _____ood the seashore.

2. Circle each prefix or suffix. Write the meaning of the underlined word.

A. The joyful bird sang from the tree branch.

_____

B. The brave butterfly was unafraid of the snake below.

_____

C. My mom was worried that the breakable lamp would be crushed to pieces.

_____

D. The catcher warmed up before the big game.

_____

E. The computer went to sleep because it was inactive for two minutes.

_____

3. Read the sentences. Divide the underlined word into syllables.

A. It is easy to comprehend why the cat was afraid of the dog.
B. My brother and I have separate bedrooms.
C. Megan had fun decorating her new backpack.
D. The class decided to celebrate the last day of school.
E. Toby's favorite flavor of ice cream is vanilla.

4. Circle the misspelled words. Write them correctly below.

What wood you do if you and a frend found money on the ground? Sum peeple mite keep it. Others would try to figure out who it belongs two. You could by a butiful new toy or a bag ful of candy. But, the wize thing to do is to return it to it's owner. What would you deside to do?

_____ _____ _____ _____ _____

_____ _____ _____ _____ _____

Word Lists

Words for Decoding

Use these lists of words when you are assessing language concepts. The lists are not comprehensive but can be used as grade-level examples for creating your own assessments, flash cards, etc.

Vowel Teams	*R*-Controlled Vowels	scr	cr	tr
ai		scramble	crab	train
brain	**ar**	scrap	crest	travel
faint	arm	scratch	cross	tragic
hail	bark	scream	crumb	troop
paid	march	scrub	crystal	truck
stain	shark	**spr**	**fl**	**Digraphs**
ea	yard	spray	flame	**ch**
beach	**er**	spread	fleet	chain
feast	brother	sprinkler	flip	cheese
meat	enter	sprout	floss	chimney
peach	hammer	spruce	flung	chose
scream	person	**str**	**fr**	chunk
ee	sister	straight	fry	**sh**
cheek	**ir**	street	Friday	shadow
knee	bird	strike	friend	sheet
queen	circle	strong	free	shirt
sleeve	first	struggle	**gl**	fresh
teeth	giraffe	**bl**	glad	trash
oa	squirt	black	glee	wish
coach	**or**	blend	glamour	**th**
goal	born	blank	glass	thank
load	horse	blow	**gr**	thorn
road	morning	bloom	great	thumb
throat	short	blue	grape	brother
ou	**ur**	**br**	grass	gather
about	burn	brag	grab	weather
bounce	curl	breeze	**pl**	bath
count	hurry	brick	plan	teeth
house	purple	bring	place	tooth
scout	turtle	broad	plaque	**initial**
ow	**Blends**	bruise	pluck	**wh**
brown	**st**	**cl**	**pr**	whale
clown	stable	claw	pride	wheat
crown	steel	clever	produce	which
flower	sting	click	proper	whiskers
mower	stone	clover	proud	whistle
shower	stung	clump	prime	why

Word Lists

Syllables
two syllables
able
butter
candle
circus
closet
dentist
dollar
drama
even
follow
funny
gallop
happy
jingle
kitten
lady
little
marry
narrow
orange
pencil
puppy
rabbit
raccoon
seven
squirrel
summer
turkey
twenty
water
winter
wonder

three syllables
addition
afternoon
beautiful
beginning
butterfly
celery
decided
elephant
eleven
eraser
evergreen
gasoline
grasshopper
hospital
however
important
magazine
negative
October
parachute
piano
potato
remember
respectful
somebody
syllable
telephone
umbrella
vacation
wonderful
xylophone
yesterday
zucchini

Homophones
aloud/allowed
ant/aunt
ate/eight
bare/bear
beet/beat
blew/blue
break/brake
buy/by/bye
dear/deer
fair/fare
feet/feat
flea/flee
flower/flour
for/four
flu/flew
groan/grown
guest/guessed
hair/hare
hear/here
herd/heard
hire/higher
in/inn
its/it's
knight/night
knot/not
mail/male
meat/meet
mist/missed
new/knew
no/know
not/knot
one/won
our/hour
pale/pail
pare/pear
passed/past

plain/plane
principal/
    principle
read/red
reel/real
right/write
rode/rowed/road
rose/rows
sail/sale
scene/seen
seem/seam
so/sew/sow
soar/sore
some/sum
son/sun
stair/stare
stake/steak
tale/tail
tea/tee
there/their/
    they're
throne/thrown
to/too/two
tow/toe
wait/weight
wail/whale
way/weigh
weather/whether
week/weak
wood/would

Irregularly Spelled Words
about
again
because
brought
buy
by
climb
color
could
design
does
enough
everybody
friendly
group
heard
hidden
into
knew
know
learn
listen
new
no
often
people
really
said
sign
their
there
they're
two

Field Trip!

Jeremy's class was going on a field trip to the beach. They were going to see the tide pools. They were going to study the plants and the animals that lived there.

Jeremy had just moved to Los Angeles from Colorado. He had seen snow, bears, and mountains, but he had never seen the ocean. He was very excited.

The morning of the field trip, Jeremy could not get out of bed. His throat was really sore. Every time he tried to stand up, the room spun around. His mother came in to see if he was ready. When she saw him still in bed, she knew something must be wrong. She felt his forehead. He was running a fever.

"I'm not going to see the beach today, am I?" Jeremy asked.

"Not today. But, don't worry. The ocean will be there when you feel better. We will go then," his mother said.

Field Trip!

Jeremy's class was going on a field trip to the beach. They were going to see the   17

tide pools. They were going to study the plants and the animals that lived there.   32

Jeremy had just moved to Los Angeles from Colorado. He had seen snow, bears,   46

and mountains, but he had never seen the ocean. He was very excited.   59

The morning of the field trip, Jeremy could not get out of bed. His throat was   75

really sore. Every time he tried to stand up, the room spun around. His mother came   91

in to see if he was ready. When she saw him still in bed, she knew something must be   110

wrong. She felt his forehead. He was running a fever.   120

"I'm not going to see the beach today, am I?" Jeremy asked.   132

"Not today. But, don't worry. The ocean will be there when you feel better. We   147

will go then," his mother said.   153

Number of Words Read	Words per Minute	Words Read in Error
First Try		
Second Try		
Third Try		

Do or Dare?

When I was four, I ate an earthworm. It wasn't because I was starving, but because of a dare. The trouble began when my sister Laura and our friend Emma said that a worm would be the worst thing to eat.

"That's not true," I said. "Lots of things are worse, such as liver and onions. Or broccoli. Or mashed turnips."

"If you think worms are so good to eat," Laura said, "prove it. Eat one! We promise we won't tell."

"You won't do it," Emma **taunted**, putting her hands behind her ears and wiggling them at me. "You're scared stiff to eat a worm. You're just a great big scaredy-cat!"

"I am not!" I answered. "I'm just not hungry!"

The girls bet that they could locate a worm. They also bet that I would not eat it, dead or alive, because I was a scaredy-cat.

Laura and Emma came dancing back from the garden with smirks on their faces, holding up a wiggling brown and pink earthworm. My stomach rolled. It was four inches long and as thick as a pencil.

"I can't eat that!" I gulped, "It's alive!"

"Scaredy-cat, scaredy-cat!" sang Laura and Emma.

So, I rinsed the poor creature off, closed my eyes, and stuck it in my mouth. It wriggled on my tongue, and I wanted more than anything to spit it out. I wondered if I should chew it.

It was already beginning to taste like something out of the garbage, so I threw back my head and swallowed. Luckily, the squirming creature was slick from the garden hose and slid right down.

That's how I came to eat a worm. I learned later that worms are an excellent source of protein. But, here's one more true fact: I've never eaten another!

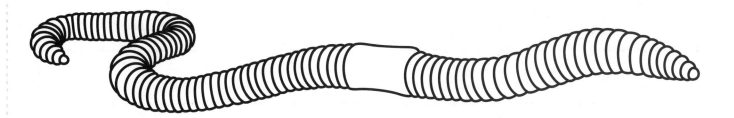

Do or Dare?

When I was four, I ate an earthworm. It wasn't because I was starving, but 15
because of a dare. The trouble began when my sister Laura and our friend Emma said 31
that a worm would be the worst thing to eat. 41

"That's not true," I said. "Lots of things are worse, such as liver and onions. Or 57
broccoli. Or mashed turnips." 61

"If you think worms are so good to eat," Laura said, "prove it. Eat one! We 77
promise we won't tell." 81

"You won't do it," Emma **taunted**, putting her hands behind her ears and 94
wiggling them at me. "You're scared stiff to eat a worm. You're just a great big 110
scaredy-cat!" 111

"I am not!" I answered. "I'm just not hungry!" 120

The girls bet that they could locate a worm. They also bet that I would not eat it, 138
dead or alive, because I was a scaredy-cat. 146

Laura and Emma came dancing back from the garden with smirks on their faces, 160
holding up a wiggling brown and pink earthworm. My stomach rolled. It was four 174
inches long and as thick as a pencil. 182

"I can't eat that!" I gulped, "It's alive!" 190

"Scaredy-cat, scaredy-cat!" sang Laura and Emma. 196

So, I rinsed the poor creature off, closed my eyes, and stuck it in my mouth. It 213
wriggled on my tongue, and I wanted more than anything to spit it out. I wondered if I 231
should chew it. 234

It was already beginning to taste like something out of the garbage, so I threw 249
back my head and swallowed. Luckily, the squirming creature was slick from the garden 263
hose and slid right down. 268

That's how I came to eat a worm. I learned later that worms are an excellent 284
source of protein. But, here's one more true fact: I've never eaten another! 297

Number of Words Read	Words per Minute	Words Read in Error
First Try		
Second Try		
Third Try		

Goliath Bird-Eating Tarantulas

The Goliath bird-eating tarantula is a spider with fangs and an attitude. They are huge, with leg spans up to 12 inches—about the same size as a dinner plate or small pizza.

These oversized, hairy spiders can be found in some South American countries. They are found in wet swamps and marshy parts of rain forests. They live in the ground. They find abandoned rodent holes or dig their own.

Goliath bird-eaters are nocturnal and stay in their holes during the day. They come out at night for food. They are good hunters and are very strong. When they find prey, they pounce and bite it with their fangs. The venom in their fangs kills the prey.

So, what's for dinner? These tarantulas like to eat lizards, small snakes, frogs, insects, bats, rats, and young birds. Tarantulas have no teeth, but their poison turns the prey into mush. Slurp!

The Goliath bird-eater is not a serious danger to people, although a bite with its one-inch fangs would hurt. It also shoots tiny hairs that make a person's skin sore. If you think one is close by, listen for a hissing noise. The sound is made as its legs are rubbed together. It can be heard as far away as 15 feet.

Although interesting, no one wants to hug or pet these creatures. They are very aggressive and do not make good pets. But, some South Americans do find a roasted Goliath bird-eating spider to be a tasty meal!

Goliath Bird-Eating Tarantulas

The Goliath bird-eating tarantula is a spider with fangs and an attitude. They are   14
huge, with leg spans up to 12 inches—about the same size as a dinner plate or small   32
pizza.   33

These oversized, hairy spiders can be found in some South American countries.   45
They are found in wet swamps and marshy parts of rain forests. They live in the ground.   62
They find abandoned rodent holes or dig their own.   71

Goliath bird-eaters are nocturnal and stay in their holes during the day. They   84
come out at night for food. They are good hunters and are very strong. When they find   101
prey, they pounce and bite it with their fangs. The venom in their fangs kills the prey.   118

So, what's for dinner? These tarantulas like to eat lizards, small snakes, frogs,   131
insects, bats, rats, and young birds. Tarantulas have no teeth, but their poison turns the   146
prey into mush. Slurp!   150

The Goliath bird-eater is not a serious danger to people, although a bite with its   165
one-inch fangs would hurt. It also shoots tiny hairs that make a person's skin sore. If you   182
think one is close by, listen for a hissing noise. The sound is made as its legs are rubbed   201
together. It can be heard as far away as 15 feet.   212

Although interesting, no one wants to hug or pet these creatures. They are very   226
aggressive and do not make good pets. But, some South Americans do find a roasted   241
Goliath bird-eating spider to be a tasty meal!   249

Number of Words Read	Words per Minute	Words Read in Error
First Try		
Second Try		
Third Try		

Fireflies

As sun goes down, lights blink on,
yellow twinkling night beams.
Summer evening, bits of gold,
fireflies flashing light dreams.

As night sky flickers brightly,
the little insects' call,
Hello! And how do you do?
Bright greetings for one and all!

The shimmering show begins now,
a dazzling, dizzy dance.
Flashes, flings, crisscross the sky
as a friendly cricket chants.

Pink dawn of morning, rising sun,
when fireflies flit away,
until dark night comes in once more
to signal their starry ballet.

Fireflies

As sun goes down, lights blink on,	7
yellow twinkling night beams.	11
Summer evening, bits of gold,	16
fireflies flashing light dreams.	20
As night sky flickers brightly,	25
the little insects' call,	29
Hello! And how do you do?	35
Bright greetings for one and all!	41
The shimmering show begins now,	46
a dazzling, dizzy dance.	50
Flashes, flings, crisscross the sky	55
as a friendly cricket chants.	60
Pink dawn of morning, rising sun,	66
when fireflies flit away,	70
until dark night comes in once more	77
to signal their starry ballet.	82

Number of Words Read	Words per Minute	Words Read in Error
First Try		
Second Try		
Third Try		

Fluency Passages: Comprehension Questions

Field Trip! (pages 45 and 46)

1. Why was Jeremy's class going to the beach?

2. What was Jeremy's problem?

3. How did Jeremy's mom know there was a problem?

4. What do you think will happen next?

Do or Dare? (pages 47 and 48)

1. Who are the main characters?

2. At what time of year do you think this story takes place?

3. What did the narrator do?

4. What does the word **taunt** mean?

Goliath Bird-Eating Tarantulas (pages 49 and 50)

1. On what continent would you find Goliath bird-eating tarantulas?

2. How large are the tarantulas?

3. Name three things tarantulas like to eat.

4. What kind of noise does the tarantula make?

Fireflies (pages 51 and 52)

1. In what time of year does "Fireflies" take place?

2. What time of day do the fireflies come out?

3. What does the metaphor "a dazzling, dizzy dance" refer to?

4. When do the fireflies flit away?

A

Turn to page _____ in your

_____ book.
List all words you find containing vowel teams.

B

Circle the correct homophone in each sentence.

1. I (ate, eight) chicken, green beans, and a roll for dinner.

2. The construction worker dug a (hole, whole) in the backyard.

3. Kim's favorite (pear, pair) of cowboy boots fit her perfectly.

4. Our class had to (wait, weight) in line at lunchtime.

5. Our soccer team finally won after an (hour, our) and a half.

C

Correct each irregularly spelled word.

peeple _____

beefor _____

evrybodee _____

favrit _____

frend _____

becawz _____

reely _____

D

Match each prefix and suffix to its meaning.

pre-	again	-less	able to
re-	not	-ly	without
un-	after	-er	one who
post-	before	-able	in the manner of

E

Write five contractions. Then, write the words used to form each.

_____ = _____ + _____

_____ = _____ + _____

_____ = _____ + _____

_____ = _____ + _____

_____ = _____ + _____

F

Draw lines to separate words with more than one syllable. Do not draw lines for words with only one syllable. Then, write the number of syllables.

1. jumping _____   **4.** bounce _____

2. outside _____   **5.** leap _____

3. exercise _____   **6.** hopping _____

Writing Prompts

Use the writing prompts to assess the class's or an individual student's proficiency with writing. Choose a card to use as a class assessment. Or, choose several cards to create a writing center for students. You can assess a student's narrative writing skills by using prompts A–L. Assess a student's opinion writing skills by using prompts M–P. Use prompts Q–W to assess a student's descriptive writing skills and prompts X–AD to assess his informative/explanatory writing skills.

Fairy tales have been around forever. Think about your favorite fairy tale. Write your own version of the story.

A

A fable is a story that teaches a moral, or lesson. Write a fable that teaches the golden rule: Treat others as you wish to be treated.

B

Title: A Crazy Day in Third Grade

Write a story that goes with this title.

C

Realistic fiction is a story that is made-up, or fiction, but that could really happen. Write a story that fits in this genre.

D

One day at recess, all of your friends start talking about the greatest new toy. The next day, they all bring that toy to school. You are the only one who doesn't have the new toy. Write a story telling what happens next.

E

Pretend that every time you sit down to watch your favorite television show, your older sister always takes the remote and changes the channel. Make a plan for how you will stop her from taking the remote next time.

F

Imagine you are walking down the hallway at school. When you get to your classroom door, it looks completely different. There is no door handle, and it is a completely different color. Write a story about what happens next. **G**

As you drift off to sleep one night, you begin to have the most amazing dream. Write a poem about your wonderful dream. **H**

Imagine it is a rainy Saturday afternoon and the power is out at your house. Write a schedule of what you would do to keep yourself busy all afternoon. **I**

Imagine it is 20 years in the future. What do you think you will be doing? What job will you have? Where will you live? Who will be your closest friend? Write a futuristic story about your life. **J**

Imagine you are walking through the woods. You walk up to a creek and see the most unusual animal swimming by. Describe the animal you see and the events that happen next. **K**

Imagine that your pencil can read your mind. Everything you think, it writes down on its own without you having to lift a finger. What would your pencil write? What do you think about this new pencil? **L**

Students have many things that they worry about every day. Write a letter to your parents, teacher, or principal explaining what worries you each day. **M**

Write a letter to your school principal convincing him or her to _____. **N**

Music, Art, or PE: which of these is your favorite? Write a letter to your best friend convincing him that it should be his favorite too.

O

Which would make a better pet: a parrot or a tarantula? Write an essay stating your point of view and why you feel the way you do.

P

Imagine you see the coolest pair of tennis shoes at the mall. Write an essay convincing your parents to buy you the new pair of shoes.

Q

Pretend your family is moving to a new house. One bedroom has an outdoor balcony, and the other has a built-in TV and game system. Write an article convincing your parents which room you should have.

R

Technology is always improving. Think about how you would improve the computer. Describe changes you would invent and make for the computer.

S

Imagine you are going to spend a week on a deserted island. You are only allowed to bring three items. There is no Wi-Fi or cell service, but there is plenty of food. What three items would you bring and why?

T

Think about the last kid's meal you ate. You have just been asked to make it better. Describe the new kid's meal you would design.

U

For your next birthday, your parents will let you design your dream cake. Draw and label a diagram of your dream cake. Then, write a descriptive paragraph about it.

V

Think about all of the amazing things you have done so far this school year. Write a song about it.

W

Think about your favorite type of technology. Write an article explaining how to use your favorite type of technology.

X

Imagine you are looking through a science textbook, and you see a picture of your favorite animal. Write an informative essay telling what you know about this animal.

Y

Think about the last new math skill you used. Write a how-to essay explaining how to use this new math skill.

Z

Think about your favorite game to play. Write an informative essay explaining how to play the game.

AA

Imagine you are a toad and you are tired of everyone confusing you for a frog. Write an essay explaining what makes you a toad and how you are different from a frog.

AB

Think about the last topic you studied in science or social studies. Write an informational newspaper article about the topic. Be sure to include a main idea with supporting details.

AC

Everyone has a favorite way to eat a sandwich. Write a how-to essay explaining the way you eat your sandwich.

AD

Revising and Editing Paragraphs

Read the paragraph. Find and circle the 16 errors. Then, correctly rewrite the paragraph on the lines. Be sure to revise as you write by improving word choice and voice.

Camping can be so much fun last weekend, me and my family went camping in a park near the mountins. We took lots of stuff because we weren't sure what we would need. Dad and I set up the tents, while Mom and my brother built a campfire and make lunch. After lunch, we went swimming in the lake. Later, we went fishing my dad cot five fish! He cleaned it and cooked them over the campfire for diner. They tasted grate! After dinner, we tosted marshmallows and tell scary storys. I wasn't really afraid. Finally, we crawled inside our tents to go to sleep. It was quite except for the crickets. The next morning, we got up and starts another day of fun. I love camping?

_____

_____

_____

_____

_____

_____

_____

_____

_____

_____

_____

_____

_____

Revising and Editing Paragraphs

Read the paragraph. Find and circle the 21 errors. Then, correctly rewrite the paragraph on the lines. Be sure to revise as you write by improving word choice and voice.

Last year was alot of fun. In january, we went skiing in denver Colorado. In february, my class performed a play about the life of martin Luther king, jr. I got to play the part of dr king. In the spring, my family spent a weak at the beech. We seen two baby sharks swiming around the fishing pier! During the summer, I visited my Grandparents in Texas. I visited the space center in houston. Finally, in december, I had the best birthday ever! I got a puppy. I named him wolf because he looks like a baby wolf. Last year was relly a lot of fun. I hope next year will be even better!

_____

_____

_____

_____

_____

_____

_____

_____

_____

_____

_____

Opinion: Students should wear uniforms to school.

Write two reasons to support this opinion.

1. _____

_____

2. _____

_____

A

Think about your opinion on how much homework students should have. Write an introduction stating your opinion.

_____

_____

_____

_____

_____

_____

B

Circle the word that best completes each sentence.

1. Kids should not watch more than one hour of television (because, therefore, for example) it can strain their eyes.

2. The glaciers continue to melt, (because, therefore, for example) the polar bears are suffering.

3. Many animals suffer when trees are cut down; (because, therefore, for example), birds lose their homes.

C

Imagine you have just written a fantastic letter to your parents convincing them to buy you a new video game. Write a strong conclusion to your letter.

_____

_____

_____

_____

_____

D

Topic: _____

Main Idea: _____

Illustration to support the main idea:

E

Topic: Dogs are animals that are easily trained by humans.

Supporting Detail: _____

_____

Supporting Detail: _____

_____

Supporting Detail: _____

_____

F

Write the word from the word bank to best complete each sentence.

| also | and | another | but | more |

1. Cats make great pets, _____ they are good companions too.

2. _____ reason cats are great is that they catch mice and bugs.

3. Many people like cats, _____ others are allergic to them.

G

Use the organizer to write a conclusion to the essay.

Introduction: Tropical rain forests are home to many different plants and animals.

| **Detail:** Sloths and glass frogs live there. | **Detail:** Many plants grow in the rain forest. | **Detail:** We must protect these plants and animals. |

Conclusion: _____

H

Plan an imaginary story.

Characters: _____

Event 1: _____

Event 2: _____

Event 3: _____

Event 4: _____

Conclusion: _____

_____

I

Write a dialogue between these two characters.

Papa Bear: _____

_____

Wolf: _____

_____

Papa Bear: _____

Wolf: _____

Papa Bear: _____

J

Use temporal words such as *first* and *next* to show the sequence of events.

_____, Matt and his two friends rode their bikes in the neighborhood.

_____, they began to get thirsty and hungry.

_____, the boys stopped at Matt's house for a snack.

_____, Matt and his friends went back out to ride bikes again.

K

Read the short story. Then, write a conclusion.

Sandra's mother offered to help her get ready for the new school year. Sandra had grown a full inch taller over the summer. Her shoes were too tight, and her pants were almost above her ankles.

Conclusion: _____

_____

_____

L

✦ Show What You Know ✦
Grammar and Conventions

Look at each underlined word. Write a word from the word bank that tells what part of speech it is.

> adjective   adverb   noun   pronoun   verb

_____ **1.** Jessica <u>quickly</u> dried her hair.

_____ **2.** <u>She</u> did not study for the test.

_____ **3.** The <u>alarm</u> rang for 20 minutes!

_____ **4.** Persian cats have <u>long</u> hair.

_____ **5.** Miguel <u>stuck</u> the marshmallow on the stick.

Circle the abstract noun in each sentence.
6. Take pride in your work.
7. A dog's loyalty to its owner is amazing.

Read the sentences. Circle the word that best completes each sentence.
8. Nikki has an (easier, easy) job than Mike.
9. The cat chased three (mouse, mice) under the barn.
10. Janelle was (study, studying) in her room.
11. Why do cows (chew, chews) their cuds?
12. Dave ate his carrots (noisier, noisily).
13. Did you see her (steal, stole) first base?

Read each sentence. Write **S** for simple, **C** for compound, and **CX** for complex. Circle each coordinating conjunction and underline each subordinating conjunction.

_____ **14.** Carmen and I went to the beach, but we didn't swim.

_____ **15.** Carmen and I went to the beach.

_____ **16.** Because the water was cold, Carmen and I did not go in.

Read the paragraph. Circle each error.
Dear Owen

    My brother and sister went to the cirkus when I was at the beach with my friend. We went swimming in the ocean every day. My friends parents took us to see the new action movie! But, I felt sad that I hadnt gone to the circus. My brother said You missed the best circus ever! Tell me what you are doing this sumer. Right to me at 548 Freeman Road Tucson Arizona, 85748.
Your friend
Cara

✦ Show What You Know ✦
Grammar and Conventions

Look at each underlined word. Write a word from the word bank that tells what part of speech it is.

> adjective   adverb   noun   pronoun   verb

_____ **1.** The plane rose <u>quickly</u> into the stormy sky.

_____ **2.** Natalie <u>helped</u> her grandmother bake bread.

_____ **3.** Carlos did not wear a <u>sweater</u> today.

_____ **4.** Nathan bought a <u>shiny</u>, new car.

_____ **5.** <u>She</u> played the song at least 10 times!

Circle the abstract noun in each sentence.
  6. The lion's braveness disappeared when the cobra hissed.
  7. The ballerina's success is due to years of practice.

Read the sentences. Circle the word that best completes each sentence.
  8. Twelve Canada (geese, goose) flew in a large vee.
  9. Yesterday, Mischa (tried, trying) hard to be the best pitcher ever.
 10. The rabbits happily (nibbles, nibble) the scraps of lettuce.
 11. Aaron looked up (quicker, quickly) when his name was called.
 12. Did you (think, thought) they would win the game?
 13. Tripp and John helped each other with (his, their) homework.

Read the sentences. Write **S** for simple, **C** for compound, and **CX** for complex. Circle each coordinating conjunction and underline each subordinating conjunction.

_____ **14.** The girls went to the mall, but they didn't do much shopping.

_____ **15.** The girls went to the mall.

_____ **16.** Because the mall was crowded, the girls did not stay for long.

Read the paragraph. Circle each error.
Dear Kevin

     This has been the best spring break! I had a lot of fun and didnt miss scool a bit. The only thing I did for school was to read a book called summer turning. My favorite sentence was The last week of august spins its wheels, over and over, finally giving in to the first days of autumn. I know just how that feels. Tell me what you are doing this sumer. Right to me at 322 Manor Road Boise Idaho 83712.

Your friend
Felicia

Name _____ Date _____

✦ Show What You Know ✦
Word Meanings

Circle the correct definition of the underlined word.

1. I used the <u>scale</u> to find out how much the fish I caught weighed.

    A. a machine used to find the weight   B. the outer covering of a fish
       of something

2. Many different plants and animals call the <u>desert</u> home.

    A. to leave   B. a dry, arid environment

3. I <u>dove</u> down to the deepest part of the swimming pool.

    A. a type of bird   B. the past tense of dive

4. The <u>fly</u> zipped around the room looking for a way out of the house.

    A. to soar through the air   B. a small insect with wings

Add the suffix **-less** or **-ness** to complete each sentence.

5. The dark_____ scared the children.

6. The shot was nearly pain_____.

7. I love the sweet_____ of a tangerine.

Answer the questions.

8. If **view** means *look at*, what does **preview** mean?

_____

9. If **port** means *to carry*, what does **deport** mean?

_____

10. If **fortunate** means *lucky*, what does **unfortunate** mean?

_____

Describe people who are

11. friendly. _____

12. helpful. _____

13. creative. _____

Name _____   Date _____

✦ Show What You Know
Word Meanings

Circle the correct definition of the underlined word.

1. After eating dinner, my dad paid the <u>bill</u>.

   A. the mouth of a bird.   B. the amount of money owed

2. I had to wear sunglasses because my <u>pupils</u> were sensitive to light.

   A. a student   B. a part of the eye

3. A feather is <u>light</u>, and a bowling ball is heavy.

   A. a source that makes it possible to see   B. having little weight

4. The horse was kept in the <u>stable</u> at night.

   A. a building in which horses are kept   B. not easily moved

Add the suffix **-able** or **-ment** to complete each sentence.

5. The weather will be favor _____ to have our picnic outside today.

6. The US govern_____ helps to make and uphold laws.

7. The brother and sister reached an agree_____ and ended their fight.

Answer the questions.

8. If **cut** means to *open* or *divide*, what does **precut** mean? _____

9. If **wise** means *smart*, what does **unwise** mean? _____

10. If **edible** means *able to eat*, what does **inedible** mean? _____

Describe people who are

11. lonely. _____

12. respectful. _____

13. unfriendly. _____

Write the meaning of each underlined phrase.

14. <u>It was raining cats and dogs</u>, so the picnic was moved inside._____

15. After winning the race, <u>he felt as bright as the sun</u>. _____

Word Lists

Words for Language Assessments

Use these lists of words when you are assessing language concepts. The lists are not comprehensive but can be used as grade-level examples for creating your own assessments, flash cards, etc.

Nouns
baby
bear
bell
corn
chicken
eyes
friend
frog
grass
orangutan
pizza
spider
tomato
umbrella

Irregular Plural Nouns
child/children
deer/deer
elf/elves
fish/fish
foot/feet
goose/geese
knife/knives
loaf/loaves
man/men
mouse/mice
ox/oxen
person/people
tooth/teeth
wolf/wolves
woman/women

Abstract Nouns
anger
bravery
care
childhood
excitement
fear
friendship
happiness
hatred
health
joy
love
luck
peace
sadness
success
talent

Adjectives
beautiful
bitter
few
furry
gigantic
lonely
one
several
short
sweet
tasty
twenty
yellow

Verbs
build
crawl
dance
destroy
explore
growl
run
scream
slither
sprint
walk
whisper
work
yell

Adverbs
angrily
carefully
cheerfully
crazily
energetically
finally
gently
gladly
happily
loudly
naturally
noisily
quickly
safely
slowly
softly
usually

Irregular Verbs
bleed/bled
burn/burnt
freeze/froze
lie/lay
rise/rose
shoot/shot
shrink/shrank
sink/sank
speed/sped
tear/tore

Subordinating Conjunctions
after
before
even though
if
once
though
until
when
while

Multiple Meaning Words
back
bat
circle
duck
fair
fly
grade
left
pitcher
ruler

Word Lists

Superlatives
big/bigger/biggest
small/smaller/smallest
pretty/prettier/prettiest
rich/richer/richest
poor/poorer/poorest
smart/smarter/
  smartest
simple/simpler/
  simplest
bright/brighter/
  brightest
quick/quicker/
  quickest
thick/thicker/thickest
light/lighter/lightest
calm/calmer/calmest

Base Words
bibl (book)
bibliography
bio (life)
biology
biography
antibiotic
camp (field)
camping
campground
cap (hold, take)
capture
capital
captain
cent (hundred)
century
cent
centipede
circum (around)
circumference
circumscribe
circumvent

cred (believe, trust)
credible
credential
cycl (circle)
bicycle
tricycle
cycle
digit (finger)
digital
digits
graph (draw, write)
telegraph
photograph
hemi (half)
hemisphere
hydr (water)
hydrant
hydrogen
hydroplane
kilo (thousand)
kilometer
kilobyte
micr (small)
microwave
microscope
ped (foot)
pedal
pedometer
pedestrian
port (carry)
portable
transport
quadr (four)
quadrilateral
quadrant
scrib (write)
scribble
manuscript
semi (half)
semicircle
semisweet

Prefixes
un-
unable
unclean
uncover
undo
undone
uneasy
uneven
unknown
unlock
unsafe
unsure
untie
untrue
unusual
unwelcome
re-
rebuild
recount
recycle
redecorate
rediscover
refill
refund
rejoin
remake
renew
reorder
repay
reread
return
rewrite

pre-
precut
prefix
prepackage
prepaid
prepare
preplan
preschool
preshrunk
preteen
pretest
prevent
preview
prewash

Suffixes
-less
careless
breathless
homeless
thoughtless
sleepless
-ful
colorful
hopeful
powerful
useful
wasteful
-able
acceptable
breakable
questionable
readable
treatable
-tion/-sion
confusion
education
erosion
exploration
mind
subtraction

Nouns and Adjectives

Circle the nouns in each sentence.

1. The king and queen had a ball one night in their kingdom.

2. The prince was looking for a princess to marry.

3. Many people came to the ball, hoping to become rich and famous.

4. The prince was sad when he couldn't find anyone to be his wife.

5. As everyone was leaving for the night, he saw a pretty girl in the corner.

6. The prince asked her to dance on the dance floor.

7. The boy and girl fell in love, and lived happily ever after.

8. The queen and king were very happy for the couple.

Write three adjectives to describe each noun.

9. knight

_____

_____

_____

10. horse

_____

_____

_____

11. queen

_____

_____

_____

12. king

_____

_____

_____

13. castle

_____

_____

_____

14. suit of armor

_____

_____

_____

Verbs and Adverbs

Cross out the words that are not verbs. Next to each verb, write an adverb to describe it.

1. skip _____

2. sing _____

3. photograph _____

4. sunglasses _____

5. sofa _____

6. smile _____

7. read _____

8. cat _____

9. building _____

10. pack _____

11. watch _____

12. sneeze _____

Choose two verb/adverb pairs from above. Use each pair in a sentence.

13. _____

_____

14. _____

_____

Name _____ Date _____

Regular and Irregular Plural Nouns

Write the plural form of each noun.

1. child

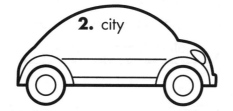
2. city

3. sheep

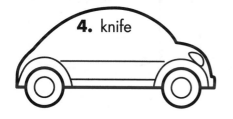
4. knife

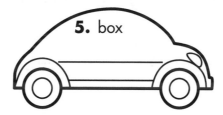
5. box

6. foot

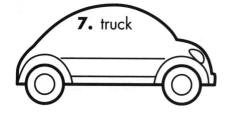
7. truck

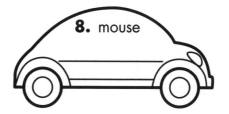
8. mouse

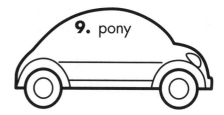
9. pony

10. half

11. couch

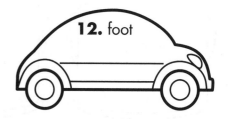
12. foot

Verb Tenses

Use the color code to color the verbs.

Color Code

present tense	=	yellow
past tense	=	orange
future tense	=	blue

paint

cleaned

will shine

worked

dry

will watch

counted

sweep

looked

will fade

cover

will name

Regular and Irregular Verbs

Write the past tense and the future tense of each word.

	Past Tense	Future Tense
1. grow	_____	_____
2. pass	_____	_____
3. come	_____	_____
4. make	_____	_____
5. give	_____	_____
6. drive	_____	_____
7. go	_____	_____
8. win	_____	_____
9. talk	_____	_____
10. draw	_____	_____
11. forgive	_____	_____
12. see	_____	_____

Subject-Verb Agreement

Underline the subject. Then, write the correct verb on the line.

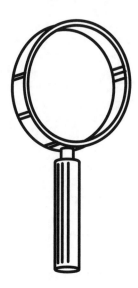

1. I _____ (work, works) as a detective, and I _____ mysteries. (solve, solves)

2. I _____ the neighborhood for mysteries. (search, searches)

3. When my friends _____ things, I help my friends find them. (lose, loses)

4. Jill _____ her cell phone often. (lose, loses)

5. My friend Juan _____ (write, writes) me coded messages and _____ them for me to find. (hide, hides)

6. I must _____ my decoder to figure them out. (use, uses)

7. My detective kit _____ me in a pinch. (help, helps)

8. I _____ helping people out. (enjoy, enjoys)

Pronoun-Antecedent Agreement

Circle the pronoun that best completes the sentence. Then, underline the antecedent it agrees with.

1. Mrs. Becker likes to give (his, her) class rewards on Friday.

2. The boys and girls like to play with (his, her, their) toys at recess.

3. Everyone should pay attention to (his, their) parents each day.

4. The guitar class students practice (their, our) instruments every day.

5. The cat likes to chase (his, its) tail and lick (her, its) paws.

6. The birds like to sing (its, their) songs in the trees.

Write the pronoun you would use in place of each subject. Then, write a sentence using both the subject and the pronoun.

7. father _____

_____

8. children _____

_____

9. wolves _____

_____

10. sun _____

_____

Simple, Compound, and Complex Sentences

Combine each pair of sentences using **and**, **or**, **but**, or **so**. Write each compound sentence on the line.

1. Our school built a playground. They opened it on April 16, 2016.

_____

2. Four days later, they opened the new soccer field. On April 20, the third grade played its first soccer game.

_____

3. The teachers took many pictures of the game. They also played in the game a little.

_____

4. You can read about the best recess ever online. You can read about it in our yearbook.

_____

5. It was the best day ever. I will remember it forever.

_____

Label each sentence as simple (**S**), compound (**C**), or complex (**CX**).

6. _____ My friends asked me to play soccer, but I do not want to play.

7. _____ The boys went to the park.

8. _____ Even though I enjoy recess, my favorite time at school is art class.

9. _____ Mary is my best friend, but I really like hanging out with Louise.

10. _____ Math is tough for me, so I have to work harder at it.

11. _____ Right now we are at lunch, so later we will go to recess.

12. _____ Everyone likes pizza with lots of cheese.

Capitalization

Write **C** if the sentence uses capitals correctly. Write **X** if the sentence does not use capitals correctly. Rewrite each sentence with an **X** correctly.

_____ **1.** "after lunch," said Reba, "let's go shopping."

_____ **2.** Taron goes to hudson elementary school in forest park.

_____ **3.** Have you visited Disneyland in California?

_____ **4.** We saw the movie *sub sandwich sleuths* yesterday.

_____ **5.** The letter to Ross ended, "Love, Aunt Rose."

_____ **6.** the hansens live in los angeles, california.

_____ **7.** In February, we went to visit Dad in Texas.

_____ **8.** "how many brothers and sisters do you have?" asked kim.

_____ **9.** My favorite TV show is *Leave it to Louis*.

_____ **10.** Today is june 10, and Tomorrow is june 11.

_____

_____

_____

_____

_____

_____

Commas

Add commas where needed in each sentence.

1. We bought bread milk and eggs at the grocery store.

2. Kim Tim Tom and Kate are all going to the birthday party.

3. The book fair will be open on Monday Wednesday and Friday.

4. The blue red yellow and green bouncy ball rolled off the table.

Cross out the sentences with incorrect punctuation.

5. Jessica was born on January 31 2008.

6. The Eiffel Tower is located in Paris, France.

7. On July 4, 1776, the United States became its own country.

8. We will travel from Los, Angeles, California to Austin, Texas.

Write two sentences using commas correctly.

9. _____

_____

10. _____

_____

Dialogue

Add correct punctuation to each sentence.

1. Eighth graders are too old to watch cartoons complained Felipe.

2. A town square is part of a town stated Olivia.

3. Enough rain can fall in one night to become a foot deep explained Felipe.

4. Mr. Walker sells the best candy in the world declared Olivia.

5. A dog is the best pet said Felipe.

6. Olivia stated Winter is the season after autumn and before spring.

7. Everyone said Felipe likes to play in the snow.

8. Olivia explained Butter will melt on a hot pan.

9. Felipe said I like the colors orange red blue and green.

10. Why are there so many clouds in the sky wondered Olivia.

Name _____ Date _____

Possessives

Add an apostrophe to each phrase to create a possessive noun. Then, complete each sentence.

1. Several astronauts spacesuits _____ .

2. The boys tennis ball _____ .

3. The three bunnies fur _____ .

4. The four cats claws _____ .

5. This weeks laundry _____ .

6. The suns rays _____ .

7. Those other girls hats _____ .

8. This robins nest _____ .

9. An elephants trunk _____ .

10. My three friends bikes _____ .

11. Those dogs owners _____ .

12. Marias glasses _____ .

13. A monkeys banana _____ .

14. Janets dimples _____ .

15. The three rabbits ears _____ .

16. Nathans truck _____ .

Name _____ Date _____

Superlatives

Write the comparative and superlative forms of each adjective.

	-er	**-est**
1. graceful	_____	_____
2. happy	_____	_____
3. good	_____	_____
4. favorite	_____	_____
5. clever	_____	_____

Use **-er** or **-est** to write the correct form of the word on each line.

6. My coat is (warm) _____ than yours.

Sally has the (warm) _____ coat in the class.

7. The (tall) _____ building in the United States is amazing to look at.

A three-story house is (tall) _____ than a two-story house.

8. The (great) _____ day of the week is Saturday.

Saturday is (great) _____ than Sunday in my opinion.

9. My sister thinks hamsters and gerbils are (smart) _____ than turtles.

I think that dogs are the (smart) _____ animals to have as pets.

10. The (hot) _____ day this year was in July.

Yesterday was (hot) _____ than today.

Name _____ Date _____

Suffixes

Use **-en**, **-ment**, and **-able** to form a word that matches each definition.

1. something that governs

_____

2. able to read

_____

3. to make harder

_____

4. to make lighter

_____

5. able to be washed

_____

6. able to be enjoyed

_____

7. something that is developed

_____

8. something that is shipped

_____

Write the meaning of each word.

9. tighten _____

10. beautiful _____

11. colorless _____

12. teacher _____

13. doubtful _____

14. careless _____

15. fillable _____

Prefixes

Add **un-**, **re-**, **pre-**, or **dis-** to each word in the word bank to complete the sentences.

agree	build	clean	cover
dress	easy	fix	heat
paid	pair	respect	school
trust	turn	view	

1. A _____ is a syllable added to the beginning of a word.

2. I _____ anyone who does not tell the truth.

3. Dan felt _____ about having the dentist pull his tooth.

4. My mother will _____ the cold pizza, and then it will taste great!

5. The dog was digging in the dirt to _____ the bones that he buried.

6. Many four-year-olds go to _____ before they go to kindergarten.

7. We bought our circus tickets early, so they are _____.

8. It is not polite to _____ your parents.

9. Leaving dirty dishes on the table is an _____ habit.

10. Did your father _____ your broken bike?

11. I must _____ these books to the library by Saturday.

12. We saw a _____ of the movie before anyone else.

13. Mary's little sister loves to dress and _____ her doll.

14. My brother and I _____ and fight a lot.

15. The boys had to _____ the tower after the dog knocked it down.

Name _____ Date _____

Spelling Rules

Complete each word using **ie** or **ei**.

1. n_____ghbor

2. rec_____ve

3. f_____ld

4. w_____gh

5. c_____ling

6. bel_____ve

Write the plural form of each word.

7. family _____

8. baby _____

9. tree _____

10. sky _____

11. body _____

12. tea _____

Rewrite each word correctly.

13. bat + ing _____

14. big + er _____

15. stop +ed _____

16. hit + er _____

17. play + ed _____

18. pet + ing _____

19. tube +ing _____

20. hop + er _____

Multiple Meaning Words

Read each sentence. Then, circle the letter for the correct definition of the underlined word as it is used in the sentence.

blow	A. hit; B. breathe out hard	**box**	A. fight; B. container
buck	A. dollar (slang); B. male deer	**drum**	A. beat or pound; B. musical instrument
peer	A. one of the same age; B. look at closely	**sharp**	A. pointed; B. alert or observant

1. <u>Bucks</u> have large, strong antlers.   A   B

2. The buck's <u>sharp</u> eyes look out for danger.   A   B

3. When in danger, a buck will <u>drum</u> the ground.   A   B

4. A buck will stand on its hind legs to <u>box</u>.   A   B

5. A buck can deliver a hard <u>blow</u> with his antlers.   A   B

6. The young deer will <u>peer</u> over the tall grass.   A   B

7. The new fence will cost 50 <u>bucks</u>.   A   B

8. Andrew and his <u>peers</u> watched the animals from a distance.   A   B

Literal and Nonliteral Meanings

Underline the figurative language in each sentence. Draw a picture showing the literal meaning of the phrase. Then, draw a picture of the nonliteral meaning of the phrase. Write a description of each picture on the lines.

1. It was raining cats and dogs outside yesterday.

Literal:	Nonliteral:

2. The test was so easy, it was a piece of cake!

Literal:	Nonliteral:

3. The thief was caught red-handed.

Literal:	Nonliteral:

A

Complete the bubble map with adjectives.

horse

B

Write an adverb to go with each verb.

1. jump _____ **2.** smile _____

3. jog_____ **4.** speak _____

Use a verb/adverb pair in a sentence.

5. _____

_____

C

Color each star with an irregular plural noun.

wolves   babies   books   children

students   tears   fish   geese

D

Label each verb as **past**, **present**, or **future**.

1. cries _____ **2.** will work_____

3. opened _____ **4.** breathes _____

5. walking _____ **6.** will stomp _____

7. typed _____ **8.** blinked_____

E

Write each verb in its correct tenses.

	Past	**Present**	**Future**
run	_____	_____	_____
sing	_____	_____	_____
write	_____	_____	_____
break	_____	_____	_____

F

Circle the subject that completes each sentence.

1. The (dog, dogs) are barking in the moonlight.

2. (I, We) am going to the park for a picnic.

3. The (class, classes) play at recess.

4. Our (child, children) is watching his favorite television show.

G

Color the nouns red and the verbs blue. If the word can be both a verb and a noun, color it purple.

wings   antenna   flower

fly

outside   grass   run

color

H

Match each noun to an adjective. Write a sentence using one of the pairs.

car   colorful   fast   boat

sleek   plane   antique   train

_____

_____

Write the pronoun for each noun.

Jacob = _____

Taylor and Susan = _____

all of us = _____

me = _____

Sally = _____

I

Write a paragraph about your day so far.

_____

_____

_____

_____

Circle the nouns. Underline the verbs. Box in the adjectives and adverbs.

J

Write a simple sentence.

_____

Write a compound sentence.

_____

Write a complex sentence.

_____

K

Correct each error.

the Elephant Sanctuary in nashville, tennessee, is home to old, sick, or abused elephants. tarra is an elephant who lives at the sanctuary. bella was a mutt who just showed up there one day in 2003. They became best friends.

L

Correct each error.
dear lamar,
I am writing from cedar point in sandusky ohio. It is the roller coaster capital of the world. I rode the roller coaster pictured on the front of this postcard. I loved it! Wish you were here.
your friend
Melissa

M

Add quotation marks where needed.

 Matt said excitedly, It's my birthday! I can't wait until my party tonight!

 Jill asked, Who is coming to your party?

 All of my friends and family, replied Matt. It is going to be great!

N

Color each adverb. Cross out each adjective.

sandy   quickly   cold   hot

happily   carefully   sunny   coolly

O

Choose four objects in your classroom. Write a sentence for each using at least one noun, adjective, verb, and adverb.

1. _____

2. _____

3. _____

4. _____

P

Rewrite each phrase using a possessive noun.

books of children _____

pet belonging to Tom _____

home of Jill and Bill _____

car of my teacher _____

gym of the school _____

Q

Add **-er** or **-est** to the bold word to complete each sentence.

big

The Super Slide is _____ than the Mega Slide.

The Double Helix Slide is the _____ of all time.

R

Draw a line to match a base word, a suffix, and a definition.

hope   en   without taste

taste   or   one who governs

govern   less   to make light

light   ful   full of hope

S

Draw a line to match a prefix, a base word, and a definition.

re   plan   to plan before

pre   living   not living

un   able   not able

non   play   play again

T

Use each multiple meaning word from the word bank twice.

> shed   spring

1. My dad asked me to put his tools out in the _____ .
2. My favorite time of year is _____.
3. Dogs _____ when they lose hair.
4. When the _____ broke, the toy wouldn't jump anymore.

U

Use each multiple meaning word from the word bank twice.

> ruler   bow

1. The _____ of the kingdom is old.
2. To draw a line, I use a _____.
3. It is polite to _____ before a king.
4. I put a huge _____ on top of the present.

V

Circle the figurative language phrases.

costs an arm and a leg   a friendly smile

crazy like a fox   raining cats and dogs

Use one of the circled phrases above in a sentence.

_____

_____

W

Rewrite each sentence using figurative language.

1. She was a fast runner. _____

_____

2. We were hungry by dinnertime. _____

_____

X

Write the meaning of the underlined phrase.

1. If you ever need me, I will be there at the <u>drop of a hat</u>.
   _____

2. Carol felt a bit <u>under the weather</u>.
   _____

3. <u>Once in a blue moon,</u> our teacher forgets to assign homework.
   _____

Y

Correct the spelling of each word. Then, write a sentence using one of the words.

familyes _____ partys _____

puppys _____

_____

_____

_____

Z

Explain why authors sometimes use nonliteral language in their writing.

_____

_____

_____

_____

AA

Write two sentences. In each sentence, use at least two adjectives. Underline the adjectives.

1. _____

   _____

2. _____

   _____

AB

Write a letter to your parents about cleaning your room. Be sure to use correct capitalization and punctuation.

_____

_____

_____

_____

AC

Book Title/Page _____
Count the number of:

_____ nouns   _____ verbs

_____ adjectives _____ adverbs

_____ prefixes   _____ suffixes

_____ multiple meaning words

_____ examples of figurative language

AD

Change three nouns to singular possessives by adding **'s**. Change three nouns to plural possessives by adding **s'**.

Examples: Sam's books, books' pages

1. _____ , _____

2. _____ , _____

3. _____ , _____

AE

Write a conversation you had with a friend yesterday. Be sure to use correct punctuation.

Me: _____

Friend: _____

Me: _____

Friend: _____

AF

Answer Key

Page 9

1. Answers will vary but may include that Grandma shows determination because she told Owen not to give up. 2. The case was dusty and in the closet. 3. He wants to learn because his dad played the trumpet. 4. B; 5. Do not give up.

Page 10

1. Answers will vary but may include that Lucy is loving because she wants to help her dog. 2. Lucy can learn to walk Jake and Jake can learn how to walk on a leash. 3. so that she can have fun with him; 4. B; 5. Ask for help when you need it.

Page 17

1. responsible, thoughtful; 2. They did not make it back before they got hungry. 3. Answers will vary. 4. The boys take longer to hike and get hungry. 5. Answers will vary.

Page 18

1. Plants grow better when there is no danger of bad weather or pests. 2. C; 3. You can control the weather, so they can grow all year. 4. The plants grow better. 5. He is excited because he goes home and wants to start a garden of his own.

Page 19

1. Their dad's birthday often falls on the same day as Father's Day. 2. Answers will vary. 3. A; 4. so they could surprise their dad; 5. Answers will vary.

Page 20

1. B; 2. She is nervous. Her palms are sweaty, and her shoes feel tight. She hopes she will not forget the words. 3. She bought her a new dress and helped her curl her hair. 4. She pats her shoulder and wishes her good luck. 5. Alicia feels calm. She sees Mom and her teacher smiling at her from the front row and knows she will do well.

Page 21

1. Her dad is moving and she and her mom will miss him. 2. She makes a photo craft for her mom and dad. 3. when she begins to make the photo project; 4. B; 5. The pictures will remind her that their family is strong.

Page 22

1. B; 2. D; 3. Line 4; 4. Chewing gum; 5. Answers will vary.

Pages 23–24

A–F. Answers will vary. G. nonliteral, nonliteral, literal; H. Answers will vary. I. book–chapter, drama–act, poem–stanza, Answers will vary. J. 2, 3, 1, 4; K. 3rd person, Answers will vary. L. Answers will vary but may include that the author may have wanted to give a clue to what Sammy's new friend looked like. (circled) fantasy; M–P. Answers will vary.

Page 25

1. They are mammals. 2. group, Answers will vary. 3. Answers will vary but may include *amazing, intelligent, friendly, social, big, excellent,* and *sound.* 4. Echolocation is sending out sound waves to locate objects. They use it to find food and other things. 5. Answers will vary.

Answer Key

Page 26

1. It is an insect. 2. phases, Answers will vary. 3. Answers will vary but may include *is*, *comes*, *spun*, *made*, *takes*, *become*, and *go*. 4. A silk shell, It uses the cocoon to change shape. 5. to give information

Page 33

1. They like the moist skin. 2. It does not rain often in the desert. 3. This text is about the saguaro cactus—what it looks like and how it grows, supporting details will vary. 4. A; 5. Animals drop the seeds from the fruit to the ground. The seeds sprout into new cacti.

Page 34

1. C; 2. Folk music was based on their songs and dance tunes. 3. People cross from one country to another and bring music styles with them. 4. People can hear music from different cultures. 5. Answers will vary.

Page 35

1. The original Olympics were held in Greece, the modern Olympics in different countries. The original Olympics were held every four years, the modern Olympics every two years. In the original Olympics, winners were given wreaths. In modern Olympics, winners are given medals. 2. 776 BC, Greece; 3. People who attend and watch on TV learn about the host country. 4. Although the Olympics have changed, the spirit remains the same. 5. D

Page 36

1. pulls things made of iron, steel, or nickel to it; 2. They will spring apart. 3. It has a magnetized needle that always points to the north pole. 4. Answers will vary. 5. A

Page 37

1. cold-blooded, and most lay eggs; 2. A cold-blooded animal that lays soft eggs in water. 3. A cold-blooded animal that lays hard eggs in nests. 4. D; 5. Answers will vary.

Page 38

1. They help you learn about the world. Answers will vary. 2. the library or the Internet; 3. No. Some of the greatest scientific discoveries were made by mistake. 4. A, C, D; 5. sequence

Pages 39–40

A. Answers will vary. B. SD, MI, SD, SD; C. first, finally, next, after, as a result, then; D. 1. the conditions outside, 2. if; E. to let you know the word is important to the topic; F. Answers will vary. G. It allows you to see what the text is about or better understand the topic. H–M. Answers will vary. N. Similar: amphibians, poison glands; Different: live in different places, different skin. O–P. Answers will vary.

Page 41

1. stood, sweater, climb, mountain, flower, thorn, tents, rafting; 2. A. preread [circle *pre*], read before; B. misspell [circle *mis*], spell wrong; C. repeat [circle *re*], say again; D. unable [circle *un*], not able; E. thoughtful [circle *ful*], full of thought; 3. A. ac/tive/ly; B. con/fus/ing; C. o/be/di/ent; D. con/vinc/ing; 4. Wednesday, clothes, wear, vacation, weather, sun, knew, buy, swimsuit, sure, should, though

Answer Key

Page 42

1. drove, beach, blanket, seashells, crab, cuddlefish, stick, drift, flood; 2. A. joyful [circle *ful*], full of joy; B. unafraid [circle *un*], not afraid; C. breakable [circle *able*], able to break; D. catcher [circle *er*], one who catches; E. inactive [circle *in*], not active; 3. A. com/pre/hend; B. sep/a/rate; C. dec/o/rat/ing; D. cel/e/brate; E. van/il/la; 4. would, friend, Some, people, might, to, buy, beautiful, full, wise, its, decide

Page 53

Field Trip!: 1. to see the tide pools; 2. He woke up sick. 3. He was still in bed. 4. Answers will vary. *Do or Dare*: 1. Laura, Emma, and the narrator; 2. spring; 3. She ate a worm; 4. tease; *Goliath Bird-Eating Tarantulas*: 1. South America; 2. 12 inches; 3. lizards, snakes, frogs, insects, bats, rats, birds; 4. hissing noise; *Fireflies*: 1. summer; 2. night; 3. how the fireflies look in the sky; 4. dawn of morning

Page 54

A. Answers will vary. B. 1. ate; 2. hole; 3. pair; 4. wait; 5. hour; C. people, before, everybody, favorite, friend, because, really; D. *pre-*/before, *re-*/again, *un-*/not, *post-*/after, *-less*/without, *-ly*/in the manner of, *-er*/one who, *-able*/able to; E. Answers will vary. F. 1. jump/ing, 2; 2. out/side, 2; 3. ex/er/cise, 3; 4. bounce, 1; 5. leap, 1; 6. hop/ping, 2

Pages 59–60

Camping can be so much fun. **Last** weekend, ~~me and~~ my family **and I** went camping in a park near the **mountains**. We took a lot of stuff because we weren't sure what we would need. Dad and I set up the tents, while Mom and my brother built a campfire and **made** lunch. After lunch, we went swimming in the lake. Later, we went fishing. **My** dad **caught** five fish! He cleaned **them** and cooked them over the campfire for **dinner**. They tasted **great**! After dinner, we **toasted** marshmallows and **told** scary **stories**. I wasn't really afraid. Finally, we crawled inside our tents to go to sleep. It was **quiet** except for the crickets. The next morning, we got up and **started** another day of fun. I love camping**!**

Page 60

A. Last year was **a lot** of fun. In **January**, we went skiing in **Denver,** Colorado. In **February**, my class performed a play about the life of **Martin** Luther **King Jr.** I got to play the part of **Dr. King**. In the spring, my family spent a **week** at the **beach**. We **saw** two baby sharks **swimming** around the fishing pier! During the summer, I visited my **grandparents** in Texas. I visited the **Space Center** in **Houston**. Finally, in **December**, I had the best birthday ever! I got a puppy. I named him **Wolf** because he looks like a baby wolf. Last year was **really** a lot of fun. I hope next year will be even better!

Pages 61–62

A–B. Answers will vary. C. 1. because; 2. therefore; 3. for example; D–F. Answers will vary. G. 1. and; 2. Another; 3. but; H–L. Answers will vary.

Answer Key

Page 63

1. adverb; 2. pronoun; 3. noun;
4. adjective; 5. verb; 6. pride; 7. loyalty;
8. easier; 9. mice; 10. studying; 11. chew;
12. noisily; 13. steal; 14. C, underlined:
but, circled: and; 15. S, circled: and;
16. CX, underlined: because, circled: and;
Dear Owen, My brother and sister went
to the **circus** when I was at the beach with
my friend. We went swimming in the ocean
every day. My **friend's** parents took us to
see the new action movie! But, I felt sad that
I **hadn't** gone to the circus. My brother
said, "You missed the best circus ever!"
Tell me what you are doing this **summer**.
Write to me at 548 Freeman Road, Tucson,
Arizona, 85748. Your friend, Cara

Page 64

1. adverb; 2. verb; 3. noun; 4. adjective; 5.
pronoun; 6. braveness; 7. success;
8. geese; 9. tried; 10. nibble; 11. quickly;
12. think; 13. their; 14. C, circled: but;
15. S; 16. CX, underlined: Because;
Dear Kevin, This has been the best spring
break! I had a lot of fun and **didn't** miss
school a bit. The only thing I did for school
was to read the book **Summer Turning**.
My favorite sentence was "The last week
of August spins its wheels, over and over,
finally giving in to the first days of autumn."
I know just how that feels. Tell me what you
are doing this **summer**. **Write** to me at
322 Manor Road, Boise, Idaho, 83712.
Your friend, Felicia

Page 65

1. A; 2. B; 3. B; 4. B; 5. darkness;
6. painless; 7. sweetness; 8. look at before;
9. carry out; 10. not lucky; 11–13. Answers
will vary.

Page 66

1. B; 2. B; 3. B; 4. A; 5. favorable;
6. government; 7. agreement; 8. open or
divide before; 9. not smart; 10. not able
to eat; 11–13. Answers will vary. 14. It was
raining heavily. 15. He felt excited.

Page 69

1. king, queen, ball, night, kingdom;
2. prince, princess; 3. people, ball;
4. prince, anyone, wife; 5. everyone,
night, girl, corner; 6. prince, her, floor;
7. boy, girl, love; 8. queen, king, couple;
9–14. Answers will vary.

Page 70

1–14. Answers will vary.

Page 71

1. children; 2. cities; 3. sheep; 4. knives;
5. boxes; 6. feet; 7. trucks; 8. mice;
9. ponies; 10. halves; 11. couches; 12. feet

Page 72

yellow: paint, dry, sweep, cover; orange:
cleaned, worked, counted, looked; blue:
will shine, will watch, will fade, will name

Page 73

1. grew, will grow; 2. passed, will pass;
3. came, will come; 4. made, will make;
5. gave, will give; 6. drove, will drive;
7. went, will go; 8. won, will win; 9. talked,
will talk; 10. drew, will draw; 11. forgave,
will forgive; 12. saw, will see

Page 74

1. I work, I solve; 2. I search; 3. friends
lose; 4. Jill loses; 5. Jaun writes, hides;
6. I use; 7. My detective kit helps; 8. I enjoy

Answer Key

Page 75

1. <u>Mrs. Becker</u>, her; 2. <u>boys and girls</u>, their; 3. <u>everyone</u>, their; 4. <u>students</u>, their; 5. <u>cat</u>, its,its; 6. <u>birds</u>, their; 7–10. Answers will vary.

Page 76

1. Our school built a playground and opened it on April 16, 2016. 2. Four days later, they opened the new soccer field, so on April 20, the third grade played its first soccer game. 3. The teachers took many pictures of the game, but they also played in the game a little too. 4. You can read about the best recess ever online, or you can read about it in our yearbook. 5. It was the best day ever, and I will remember it forever. 6. C; 7. S; 8. CX; 9. C; 10. CX; 11. C; 12. S

Page 77

1. "After lunch," said Reba, "let's go shopping." 2. Taron goes to Hudson Elementary School in Forest Park. 3. C; 4. We saw the movie *Sub Sandwich Sleuths* yesterday. 5. C; 6. The Hansens live in Los Angeles, California. 7. C; 8. "How many brothers and sisters do you have?" asked Kim. 9. My favorite TV show is *Leave It to Louis*. 10. Today is June 10, and tomorrow is June 11.

Page 78

1. We bought bread, milk, and eggs at the grocery store. 2. Kim, Tim, Tom, and Kate are all going to the birthday party. 3. The book fair will be open on Monday, Wednesday, and Friday. 4. The blue, red, yellow, and green bouncy ball rolled off the table. 5. incorrect; 6. correct; 7. correct; 8. incorrect; 9–10. Answers will vary.

Page 79

1. "Eighth graders are too old to watch cartoons," complained Felipe. 2. "A town square is part of a town," stated Olivia. 3. "Enough rain can fall in one night to become a foot deep," explained Felipe. 4. "Mr. Walker sells the best candy in the world," declared Olivia. 5. "A dog is the best pet," said Felipe. 6. Olivia stated, "Winter is the season after autumn and before spring." 7. "Everyone," said Felipe, "likes to play in the snow." 8. Olivia explained, "Butter will melt on a hot pan." 9. Felipe said, "I like the colors orange, red, blue, and green." 10. "Why are there so many clouds in the sky?" wondered Olivia.

Page 80

1. astronauts'; 2. boy's; 3. bunnies'; 4. cats'; 5. week's; 6. sun's; 7. girls'; 8. robin's; 9. elephant's; 10. friends'; 11. dogs'; 12. Maria's; 13. monkey's; 14. Janet's; 15. rabbits'; 16. Nathan's; Completed sentences will vary.

Page 81

1. more graceful, most graceful; 2. happier, happiest; 3. better, best; 4. more favorite, most favorite; 5. cleverer, cleverest; 6. warmer, warmest; 7. tallest, taller; 8. greatest, greater; 9. smarter, smartest; 10. hottest, hotter

Page 82

1. government; 2. readable; 3. harden; 4. lighten; 5. washable; 6. enjoyable; 7. development; 8. shipment; 9. to make tight; 10. full of beauty; 11. without color; 12. one who teaches; 13. full of doubt; 14. without care; 15. able to fill

Answer Key

Page 83

1. prefix; 2. distrust; 3. uneasy; 4. reheat;
5. uncover; 6. preschool; 7. prepaid;
8. disrespect; 9. unclean; 10. repair;
11. return; 12. preview; 13. undress;
14. disagree; 15. rebuild

Page 84

1. ei; 2. ei; 3. ie; 4. ei; 5. ei; 6. ie;
7. families; 8. babies; 9. trees; 10. skies;
11. bodies; 12. teas; 13. batting;
14. bigger; 15. stopped; 16. hitter;
17. played; 18. petting; 19. tubing;
20. hopper

Page 85

1. B; 2. B; 3. A; 4. A; 5. A; 6. B;
7. A; 8. A

Page 86

1–3. Answers will vary.

Pages 87–90

A–B. Answers will vary. C. wolves, children, fish, geese; D. 1. present; 2. future; 3. past; 4. present; 5. present; 6. future; 7. past; 8. past; E. ran, runs, will run; sang, sings, will sing; wrote, writes, will write; broke, breaks, will break; F. 1. dogs; 2. I; 3. classes; 4. child; G. fly–purple; wings–red; antenna–red; color–purple; outside–red; grass–red; flower–red; run–blue; H. Answers will vary. I. he, they, we, I, she; J–K. Answers will vary. L. **The** Elephant Sanctuary in **Nashville, Tennessee**, is home to old, sick, or abused elephants. **Tarra** is an elephant who lives at the sanctuary. **Bella** was a mutt who just showed up there one day in 2003. They became best friends. M. **Dear Lamar**, I am writing from **Cedar Point** in **Sandusky, Ohio**. It is the roller coaster capital of the world. I rode the roller coaster pictured on the front of this postcard. I loved it! Wish you were here. **Your Friend,** Melissa; N. Matt said excitedly, "It's my birthday! I can't wait until my party tonight!" Jill asked, "Who is coming to your party?" "All of my friends and family," replied Matt. "It is going to be great!" O. sandy, adjective; quickly, adverb; cold, adjective; hot, adjective; happily, adverb; carefully, adverb; sunny, adjective; coolly, adverb; P. Answers will vary. Q. children's books, Tom's pet, Jill and Bill's home, my teacher's car, school's gym; R. bigger, biggest; S. hopeful–full of hope, tasteless–without taste, governor–one who governs, lighten–to make light; T. replay–play again, preplan–to plan before, unable–not able, nonliving–not living; U. 1. shed, 2. spring, 3. shed, 4. spring; V. 1. ruler, 2. ruler, 3. bow, 4. bow; W. costs an arm and a leg, crazy like a fox, raining cats and dogs, Sentences will vary. X. Answers will vary. Y. 1. quickly, 2. feeling bad; 3. occasionally; Z. families, parties, puppies, Answers will vary.
AA. Answers will vary but may include: Authors use figurative language to make their writing more interesting to the reader.
AB–AF. Answers will vary.